H A N D B O O K O f
Differentiated Instruction Using the Multiple Intelligences

HANDBOOK OF
Differentiated Instruction Using the Multiple Intelligences
Lesson Plans and More

Bruce Campbell

PEARSON

A and B

BOSTON   NEW YORK   SAN FRANCISCO   MEXICO CITY   MONTREAL   TORONTO
LONDON   MADRID   PARIS   HONG KONG   SINGAPORE   TOKYO   CAPE TOWN   SYDNEY

Series Editor: Arnis Burvikovs
Editorial Assistant: Anne Whittaker
Director of Professional Development: Alison Maloney
Marketing Manager: Danae April
Production Editor: Gregory Erb
Composition Buyer: Linda Cox
Manufacturing Buyer: Linda Morris
Composition & Full Service Project Management: NK Graphics/Black Dot Group
Cover Coordinator: Kristina Mose-Libon

Between the time website information is gathered and then published, it is not unusual for some sites to have closed. Also, the transcription of URLs can result in typographical errors. The publisher would appreciate notification where these errors occur so that they may be corrected in subsequent editions.

ISBN-10: 0-205-56921-8
ISBN-13: 978-0-205-56921-2

Library of Congress Cataloging-in-Publication Data

Campbell, Bruce, 1945–
    Handbook of differentiated instruction using the multiple intelligences: lesson plans and more / Bruce Campbell.—1st ed.
        p.   cm.
    ISBN 0-205-56921-8 (alk. paper)
    1. Individualized instruction—Handbooks, manuals, etc.   2. Multiple intelligences—Handbooks, manuals, etc.   I. Title.
    LB1031.C346   2008
    371.39'4—dc22

                                    2007038709

Printed in the United States of America
10 9 8 7 6 5 4 3 2 1   EDW   11 10 09 08 07

To Linda Campbell and Howard Gardner,
I extend my deepest thanks. I thank my wife Linda
for her love of learning and of me.

I thank Dr. Gardner for his ongoing inspiration and support.
His Theory of Multiple Intelligences has articulated what many
teachers intuitively know—that each child is capable. In so doing,
he has provided a framework for revisioning education so that
all students can succeed.

This book is dedicated to every teacher who instills
a love of learning in students.

Brief Contents

Contents

PART IV

Differentiating Assessment in an MI Classroom 54

PART V

Differentiated Lessons Using MI 66

Preface

Welcome to the Handbook of Differentiated Instruction Using the Multiple Intelligences! *This handbook has emerged from my years of teaching through the Multiple Intelligences in an elementary, multi-age classroom. I wrote this book to share with other teachers what I have learned. I will begin with a story about one of my students named Richard and then briefly introduce Howard Gardner's Theory of Multiple Intelligences in the section that follows.*

Richard's Breakthrough

"Mr. Campbell! Mr. Campbell! Come over to the Ray Charles Center and listen to what Richard taught us."

"Okay, just a second."

"No, this is really good! You have to come right now!"

I let Kristina finish the paragraph she was reading to me and moved to the classroom music center. A group of four students—two fifth graders, a fourth grader, and Richard, a third grader—were working with a small keyboard and hand-made percussion instruments on what we called a two-part rhythm.

At the time, we were studying cells, the building blocks of life, and the way many cells in the body divide at the same time. To develop this concept musically, the students at the Ray Charles Center were creating rhythmic accompaniment to lyrics about mitosis.

As I arrived, the group explained that Richard had taught them to play an intricate three-part rhythm. This lively and inviting composition was completely of the group's creation. Soon, the whole class (not easily distracted, since students are used to lots of daily activity) had gathered around. The piece went on for about four minutes. The class stood in awe. No group had composed such complex music and this was clearly beyond anything I had suggested or demonstrated. In fact, it was well beyond anything I knew how to do.

As the composition reached a crescendo and ended with a natural cadence, the class spontaneously erupted in applause. They all recognized good music created right in their own classroom.

Most remarkable was Richard's role in the development of the composition. Richard had difficulty in nearly all subject areas—he had been identified for pull-out programs and labeled a special education student. What was surprising about his role as primary composer at the Ray Charles Center was that nobody, including Richard himself, had known he was musically proficient. What we witnessed was the sudden unfolding of a unique musical talent.

Richard had had no musical training at home or at school other than his daily work at the Ray Charles Center. After five months of working with music in the classroom, Richard discovered an inherent talent. His classmates, duly impressed, congratulated him. Their praise was a new experience for someone who had rarely been successful.

Over the next few days, Richard's musical accomplishments continued. Soon students from other classes were coming to listen. Interestingly, Richard himself began to change—he carried himself with more pride, and he began taking academic risks that he would have previously avoided.

By the end of the school year, Richard had grown in many ways. I ran into him one day in the middle of the summer vacation. He was exuberant as he told me he had his own keyboard and was "making music like mad." This was not the same reticent, withdrawn, third grader I had met just ten months earlier.

Richard's story might be more dramatic than some, but it's not unusual in a Multiple Intelligences classroom. When students learn in diverse ways on a daily basis, they frequently experience breakthroughs. Such breakthroughs include identifying areas of strength, using strengths to overcome weaknesses, discovering a love of learning, and even scoring well on standardized tests!

This book was written to assist teachers who are interested in working with the Multiple Intelligences in their classrooms. It is based on my seven years of experience teaching through the Multiple Intelligences. This book is written as a direct response to the teachers who have asked me "How do we start?" "What resources do we need?" And most commonly, "Do you have MI lesson plans to share?"

The *Handbook of Differentiated Instruction Using the Multiple Intelligences* does not cover everything you will ever need to know about the Multiple Intelligences, but it is a useful tool to help you with your efforts to teach to the strengths of each student. Good luck!

Bruce Campbell

Introduction

Getting Acquainted with Differentiated Instruction

What is differentiated instruction? There are many definitions that describe differentiated instruction as a course of action for teaching students of differing abilities in the same class. It is an approach designed to strategically meet the needs of every student. It is also a student-centered method of learning that relies on proven practices to improve students' achievement. It is a different way of thinking and planning that addresses the needs of the broad range of students in today's classrooms.

While the phrasing may be new, the concept is not. Ever since the days of the one-room schoolhouse, teachers have worked to accommodate a broad range of students' abilities and needs simultaneously. Sometimes referred to as multi-level, multi-modal, tiered, or layered instruction, differentiation simply refers to teachers' intentional efforts to improve learning for students in mixed-ability classrooms by using a variety of learning strategies.

Sometimes it is more revealing to look at what something isn't, in order to understand it. First, differentiation isn't just one thing; it includes many techniques. It's also not a specific program; it must change to meet the needs of every classroom. It's not ability grouping; it draws on the individual and collective strengths of all students. Finally, it's not a goal; teachers don't differentiate for the sake of differentiation—they differentiate to improve their students' learning and achievement.

Differentiated instruction is not a method or a strategy. As noted, it is a way of thinking and planning. It involves thinking about the different levels of readiness and ability, different students' interests, and different learning profiles. It means thinking about how to provide multiple entry points into content areas, so that all students can be successful in their studies. It means thinking about students both individually and collectively—their life experiences and their circumstances. It also means thinking about how teachers can develop meaningful relationships with students, so that students trust educators to provide meaningful learning experiences for them. Above all, it means thinking about how teachers can provide enriched learning environments that offer a variety of resources and experiences to optimize learning. I think teachers intuitively differentiate, but I also think there's always room to become more conscious of and more intentional about how to do it.

Carol Tomlinson, in her extensive writing about differentiated instruction (1995, 1999, 2003) emphasizes how to differentiate content, process, and product (curriculum, instruction, and assessment). She points out that teachers can also differentiate according to the different learning modalities or profiles of each student. So this book provides all of these: multiple resources, multiple ways for students to access the content and skills they need, multiple ways for them to express their learning, and multiple opportunities to learn through different modalities or intelligences.

Tomlinson (1999) also emphasizes the importance of small, flexible learning groups, the term *flexible grouping* frequently emerging in discussions about differentiated instruction. She also talks about the importance of mixed-ability grouping (Tomlinson 1995, 1999). Throughout the literature on effective instruction (Marzano 2003, 2004), the same ideas emerge: flexible grouping, mixed-ability grouping, a variety of resources and materials, flexible pacing, and learner-centered instruction. All of these are central to the Multiple Intelligences–based model of differentiated instruction presented in this book.

In the many other books and articles addressing differentiation, we find an array of teaching approaches, including flexible grouping, project-based learning, teaching to learning styles, problem-based learning, curriculum compacting, tiered instruction, self-directed learning, and more. Because differentiated instruction can include so many strategies, it is not easy to grasp exactly how to differentiate. That's why I've focused on Multiple Intelligences in my teaching and in this book. I think MI is the best framework available for designing differentiated lessons. It is a multi-modal approach that allows students to work on the same skills and concepts but from multiple entry points. This approach increases the likelihood that teachers will be able to help students succeed.

This book offers lots of differentiated lessons designed explicitly around Multiple Intelligences. Every lesson in this book provides eight of these entry points—in other words, eight ways to teach the targeted skill or knowledge. However, the purpose is not to use every intelligence in every lesson, but rather to determine which intelligences—which entry points—will work best for which students. This flexibility allows the teacher to pick and choose and remember that students learn in different ways.

Finally, a note about standards: In Part V, "Differentiated Lessons Using MI," I have included general standards that each lesson addresses. Schools today are standards-based and standards-driven. For better or for worse, each state (except Iowa) has its own state standards. It is beyond the scope of this book to identify specific standards for every lesson from every state; however, I take into account the standards of many states, as well as the foundational standards of organizations like the National Council for the Teaching of Mathematics. As such, the standards identified for the lessons in this book are generically based on a combination of multiple states and national organizations. I happen to think that standards are a good thing, but I also think that there are many ways to reach them. This book is an example of how teachers can reach those standards by using Multiple Intelligences to differentiate instruction. The following pages present an array of differentiated lessons, activities, and assessment processes that will engage both teachers and students. I hope they are enjoyable to work with.

Getting Acquainted with Multiple Intelligences as a Strategy for Differentiation

Before explaining what I have learned about differentiating instruction through Multiple Intelligences, I think it is important to acknowledge

Howard Gardner, a cognitive psychologist at Harvard University. In 1983 his groundbreaking book, *Frames of Mind: The Theory of Multiple Intelligences*, was first published. His work expanded the traditional notion of intelligence beyond linguistic and mathematical competencies, and redefined what intelligence is. According to Gardner, human intelligence consists of three components: a set of skills that enables an individual to resolve genuine problems encountered in life; the ability to create an effective product or offer a service that is of value in one's culture; and the potential for finding or creating problems that enables an individual to acquire new knowledge.

To arrive at this enhanced view of intelligence, Gardner studied the cognitive profiles of gifted children, people from diverse cultures, savants, and individuals who had suffered brain damage. He realized that intelligence was expressed in multiple forms. In addition to linguistic and logical–mathematical abilities, he initially identified kinesthetic, visual–spatial, musical, interpersonal, and intrapersonal intelligences. Thirteen years later he added to these original seven the intelligence of the naturalist. All eight are described below.

Linguistic intelligence is the ability to think in words and to use language to express and appreciate complex meanings. Linguistic intelligence allows humans to understand the order and meaning of words, and to apply meta-linguistic skills to reflect on their use of language. Linguistic intelligence is the most widely shared human competence and is best modeled by poets, novelists, journalists, and effective public speakers.

Logical–mathematical intelligence is the ability to calculate, quantify, consider propositions and hypotheses, and carry out complex mathematical operations. It enables us to perceive relationships and connections, to use abstract, symbolic thought, sequential reasoning skills, and inductive and deductive thinking processes. Logical intelligence is usually well developed in mathematicians, scientists, and detectives.

Bodily–kinesthetic intelligence is the capacity to manipulate objects and use a variety of physical skills. This intelligence also involves a sense of timing, and the perfection of skills through mind–body union. Athletes, dancers, surgeons, and craftspeople exhibit highly developed kinesthetic intelligence.

Spatial intelligence is the ability to think in three dimensions. Core capacities of this intelligence include mental imagery, spatial reasoning, image manipulation, graphic and artistic skills, and an active imagination. Sailors, pilots, sculptors, painters, and architects all exhibit spatial intelligence.

Musical intelligence is the capacity to discern pitch, rhythm, timbre, and tone. This intelligence enables one to recognize, create, reproduce, and reflect on music, as demonstrated by composers, conductors, musicians, vocalists, and sensitive listeners. Interestingly, there is often an affective connection between music and the emotions, and mathematical and musical intelligences may share common thinking processes.

Interpersonal intelligence is the ability to understand and interact with others effectively. It involves effective verbal and nonverbal communication, the ability to note distinctions among others, a sensitivity to the moods and temperaments of others, and the ability to entertain multiple perspectives. Teachers, social workers, actors, and politicians all exhibit interpersonal intelligence.

Intrapersonal intelligence is the capacity to understand oneself, one's own thoughts and feelings, and to use such knowledge in planning and directing one's own life. Intrapersonal intelligence involves not only an appreciation of the self, but also of the human condition, and is evident in psychologists, spiritual leaders, and philosophers.

Naturalist intelligence has to do with observing, understanding and organizing patterns in the natural environment; for example in plant development, animal behavior, cloud formation, and rock structures. A naturalist is someone who shows expertise in the recognition and classification of plants and animals. This could be anyone from a molecular biologist to a traditional medicine man using herbal remedies. These same skills of observing, collecting, and categorizing might also be applied in the "human environment," as witnessed in a child sorting sports cards, or in an adult who shrewdly distinguishes between the sounds of different engines or analyzes variations in fingerprints.

These eight intelligences provide a foundation for differentiating instruction. Accepting the notion that individuals have diverse cognitive profiles means accepting that instruction must change to accommodate them. If teachers provide multiple entry points into a content area—that is, differentiate instruction by using the Multiple Intelligences Gardner has identified—then more students can learn and be successful. Students deserve opportunities to work from their strengths, to enhance their areas of weakness, and to discover what they enjoy and love to do. This book is dedicated to nurturing the gifts of each child.

Preparing the Classroom for Differentiated Instruction

Part I addresses how to start a differentiated-instruction program using Multiple Intelligences.

In this section you will find descriptions of several classroom models that use Multiple Intelligences to differentiate instruction. The descriptions are included to show a variety of ways in which MI may be infused into your classroom instruction. I next describe my own classroom because teachers often request additional information on the learning centers I have developed. This includes how I group students for center work. Part I closes by suggesting steps to start an MI-based, differentiated program and by identifying some resources to gather. This initial section includes:

Part I Contents

- Diverse Models for Using Multiple Intelligences to Differentiated Instruction
- Daily Format in One Differentiated Classroom Using MI Learning Centers
- To—With—By
- Using Multiple Intelligences Centers to Differentiate
- Grouping Students for MI Centers
- Starting a Multiple Intelligences Program
- Resources for Differentiated, Multiple Intelligences Learning Environment

Diverse Models for Using Multiple Intelligences to Differentiate Instruction

There are many ways to set up the classroom for differentiated instruction. Each teacher must determine which classroom configuration, management system, daily schedule and which intelligences to incorporate for a given lesson. All of this depends on what is most appropriate for that teacher's teaching style, grade level, and subject area. More importantly, each teacher must determine the readiness, abilities, interests, and learning profiles of students when setting up the classroom for differentiated instruction.

Six or More Learning Centers Each Day

This model features multiple learning centers, each dedicated to one of Gardner's intelligences. The curriculum is thematic and interdisciplinary—students move from center to center learning about a particular topic in as many as eight ways. One advantage of this model is that it keeps group sizes small.

The purpose of this model is not to have new activities at each center every day. Rather, the activities at one or more of the centers may last several days or even weeks. Students continue their work each time they rotate back to that center.

Three to Five Learning Centers Each Day

This model is similar to the one above. Often activities designed to incorporate the two personal intelligences (interpersonal and intrapersonal) are de-emphasized because they are already integrated into activities at other centers. One variation is to rotate the intelligence centers from day to day or week to week—for example, students would rotate between the Music and Kinesthetic Centers. In other words, different intelligences are emphasized at different times. This model provides flexibility for the teacher and still offers multiple options for students.

Learning Centers Once Weekly

In this model five to eight centers are set up only one or two days per week. A special topic would be studied at each of the centers on these days, with a return to more traditional classroom instruction the rest of the week. This method involves more set-up and take-down time, but it is an excellent way for teachers to experiment with differentiation through MI.

Whole Class Moves Together to Different Classrooms

This is an interesting elementary model based on team-teaching. The teachers remain in separate classrooms with students moving as a whole class from room to room every forty to sixty minutes. The curriculum is interdisciplinary, with students learning about the topic from two or more teachers. Teachers serve as "intelligence experts" and co-plan their units, with each contributing in one or more areas of individual strength.

Whole-Class Instruction in Multiple Ways

This model features a traditional classroom environment with more direct instruction initially plus regular learning activities that include musical, kinesthetic, visual, interpersonal, and intrapersonal techniques. This model is probably the easiest way for teachers to bring differentiation into the classroom with Multiple Intelligences.

One Intelligence Is Emphasized

This model is a variation of the whole-class approach—the teacher highlights one intelligence per day. For example, on Monday the teacher might ask students to work together in a variety of cooperative learning strategies, to engage interpersonal intelligence. On Tuesday students might learn visually by graphing or drawing the content of that day's lessons. Over the course of several school days, each student would have opportunities to learn through several intelligences. This book provides concrete activities for each intelligence that can be adapted for any grade or subject. Some teachers using this model include an extra day in the cycle—on this day students choose to learn in the mode they each prefer.

Self-Directed Learning: Students' Choices Based on Individual Strengths

In this approach students have opportunities to pursue projects of their choice. Students plan their learning activities, frequently using Student Learning Contracts (see sample contract in the independent projects section). They set goals, create time lines, conduct independent research, and determine how to demonstrate their learning for assessment. The teacher serves as a facilitator and resource person. This approach can be used occasionally—perhaps twice quarterly at the secondary level—or it can be a regular feature of each elementary school day.

Apprenticeship Programs

There are numerous apprenticeship options that assist students in developing in-depth skills. Teachers can ask parent or community volunteers to share their expertise with small groups of students. For example, on Tuesdays three community members—a journalist, a pianist, and an actor—might work with students interested in their specialties. Some school-wide apprenticeship programs feature once-weekly or once-monthly options for the entire student body. If an individual teacher or an entire school is interested in apprenticeships, it is important to structure these apprenticeships to span several months at a time. In this way, students develop extensive knowledge and skills in a particular intelligence area.

Daily Format in One Differentiated Classroom Using MI Learning Centers

For many years I have implemented an MI classroom model that includes eight learning centers based on Gardner's original eight intelligences, and a thematic, integrated curriculum. Each center, or work station, is dedicated to one of the original eight intelligences. I have experimented by combining the two personal intelligences, leaving only six centers, and integrated both personal intelligences into other centers, leaving only five. I do not feel that it is necessary to have a designated number of centers; it is more important to provide multiple entry points into the content area. For this reason I have varied the number of centers from year to year based on what works best for that group and that grade level.) During the morning students learn about the day's topic at several centers. In the afternoon they work on self-selected projects and apply their diverse learning skills to areas of individual interest. This classroom model works well for me, but it is certainly not the only effective MI approach. The description below of how I conduct my classroom is offered as a glimpse into one MI program's daily schedule.

Opening

After the morning's attendance and announcements, I lead the students in a short discussion. This "warm-up" typically involves a news event, a current school problem, or a controversial social issue. Students are challenged to form opinions, to question each other's points of view, and to substantiate their own statements. The discussion is brief and lively.

Main Lesson

After our morning warm-up, I teach what I call my "main lesson." Students are required to take notes in their journals or notebooks on each day's main lesson. The lesson consists of a ten- to fifteen-minute overview of the subject or topic being studied For example, in a unit about outer space, the morning lesson might be on comets and what causes their elongated orbits. The lesson usually includes visuals and hands-on activities. Occasionally, it can be taught by a student who has volunteered, a parent with some expertise, or someone from the community with interest in the topic. The main lesson sets a context for the activities that follow in the learning centers. Every main lesson is derived from specific state standards/district curriculum standards.

Directions

I then give brief directions for the activities at each of the learning centers. Because some of the center-based activities are continued from the previous day, only two or three directions might be given.

Center Work

The center work is where the lesson is truly differentiated. Students move in small groups through the learning centers. Center work is structured and content-focused, but decentralized. With three to five students in each group, the students rotate through the centers. Depending on the grade level and the time of year, the groups may spend anywhere from ten to thirty minutes in each center. The skills or knowledge targeted in the main lesson is what the students now learn about in differentiated ways. Students stay with their groups and move when the teacher rings a small bell after the designated amount of time has passed. Work in the centers provides time for both collaborative and independent learning. Again, the learning activities are built around state standards. Textbooks are integrated as much as possible. In addition to curricular content, students develop diverse thinking skills; there is a strong emphasis on literacy.

While some teachers may look at the various centers and see a great amount of planning, planning time is minimized by two factors: first, students start at new centers only once a week; second, many center-based activities continue for several days or even weeks. Fridays often feature "free centers," which the students plan themselves. Free centers also provide students with opportunities to complete the week's unfinished work and to focus on areas of particular interest.

Sharing

After working at the centers, students gather as a whole group to share their learning and to receive feedback from their peers. Students volunteer or are asked to sing songs, perform skits, read aloud written work, or show art projects to the rest of the class. Students offer compliments and constructive criticism to the presenters. Daily sharing typically requires between five and fifteen minutes, and concludes the first half of the school day.

Math

The afternoon begins with a math lesson I teach to the whole class. To differentiate my math instruction, I use a combination of manipulatives to teach concepts as well as to drill and practice activities. The math lesson is usually between forty-five and sixty minutes long and is enriched by activities in the Math Center on subsequent mornings.

Projects

Next, students work on their independent projects for approximately one hour daily. Students choose their own topics and learn about them individually or in pairs. Project work is organized via a student-teacher contract that specifies what students will accomplish and when. Students are expected to become "junior experts" and to teach others what they have learned. They identify their topics, research them, and prepare a multimodal presentation for the rest of the class. Each project requires three to four weeks of student preparation. When students share their projects with the rest of the class, their presentations reveal the learning skills they have gained at the centers, as well as the knowledge they have acquired from their research. The presentations also demonstrate that students can identify their interests, set goals, and achieve them in self-directed ways.

I think that project-based learning is another powerful strategy to differentiate instruction. Considerable training and scaffolding goes into the development of good projects. I begin the year with mini-projects—one-dimensional investigations and presentations—then proceed to increasingly complex research and demonstrations of understanding. Even kindergartners and first graders can do these projects. They may need more structure, but they are fully capable of selecting an animal, a season, an author, a book, a neighborhood, or a pet, then finding out about that animal, etc., and presenting their findings to the class. At all ages the process teaches thinking skills, planning, and self-direction.

Review

At the end of the day I conduct a brief review of our main lesson, of work done in the learning centers, and of project efforts. I may also assign homework during the review, as well as preview the next day's main lesson. For example, I might say, "Today, we learned about comets and their strange orbits around the sun. What are other objects that orbit the sun?... Tomorrow's lesson will be on asteroids." The preview serves as a bridge connecting one day's lesson with the next day's. It also weaves together the unit subject area as a whole and the individual lessons.

To–With–By

I have always thought of this model as To–With–By: I teach something *to* my students (during the main lesson), I work *with* my students, providing guided instruction (in the learning centers), and then I encourage them to work more *by* themselves, or independently (on the projects). This model, whether or not it incorporates Multiple Intelligences, is differentiated in terms of the scaffolded instructional process. Incorporating Multiple Intelligences—either in learning centers or during whole-group instruction—provides further differentiation and more opportunities for students to succeed.

Note: The schedule is more flexible than it may appear. I have taught in schools with a ninety-minute reading block in the morning and worked my schedule around that. I have had PE, music, library time, and assemblies that I have had to incorporate into the schedule. There are short weeks and half days, so I am always adjusting. The important thing is that students have lots of opportunities to learn in differentiated ways. This meets the different needs, abilities, and interests of the students.

Using Multiple Intelligences Centers to Differentiate

Initially, when I began differentiating through MI learning centers, I identified each with a name that emphasized its function. For example the center for kinesthetic intelligence was called the Building Center. The visual center was called the Art Center, and so on. At the start of the second year of my MI program, a student teacher suggested that the centers be named after famous people who exhibited each of the intelligences. Together we thought about whom the centers might feature and generated a list of exemplary individuals. I have named the centers after famous individuals every year since, and it is an idea that has caught on with many educators around the country.

Highlighting such intelligence experts at the centers offers numerous curricular possibilities. My students spend the first week of school learning about the Multiple Intelligences and these exemplary individuals. After learning about such people, how they developed their skills, and the contributions they made, the students begin to expect that their own capacities will develop over time and that they can, too, make contributions. Another phenomenon I have observed is that students begin to identify with certain individuals. It is almost as if the MI "geniuses" begin to serve as mentors in absentia for my students. Also, when an individual student exhibits particularly strong skills, her classmates may refer to her as the class's Picasso or Emily Dickinson.

I change the names of my centers each year. For example, the kinesthetic center has changed from Thomas Edison to Martha Graham. When the center was named for Thomas Edison, I provided a variety of building and inventing activities. With the change to Martha Graham, I emphasize creative movement and dance. The center names guide my curriculum planning throughout the year. My MI centers are currently dedicated to the following people:

William Shakespeare Center	Linguistic Intelligence
Albert Einstein Center	Logical–Mathematical Intelligence
Martha Graham Center	Kinesthetic Intelligence
Pablo Picasso Center	Visual–Spatial Intelligence
Ray Charles Center	Musical Intelligence
Mother Teresa Center	Interpersonal Intelligence
Emily Dickinson Center	Intrapersonal Intelligence
Jane Goodall Center	Naturalist Intelligence

Numerous teachers have experimented with names for their centers. One teacher named the centers after teachers in her building, another after famous women, and a third after fictional characters. A fourth named the centers after members of the community who served as classroom mentors by regularly visiting the school and sharing their expertise with students. Some teachers change center names during the year, while others encourage their students to choose center names on a quarterly basis.

Grouping Students for MI Centers

I am often asked how I group my students for their work at the learning centers. The following procedures are the ones I rely on when composing student groups. These guidelines can be used in classrooms with learning centers or for cooperative learning in classrooms without centers. As the teacher I assume responsibility for creating student groups. Toward the end of the school year, however (when their social skills are better developed), students may select their own group members. Groups typically consist of three, four, or five students and are composed according to the following considerations:

1. **Mixed-ability grouping:** I intentionally mix students together who have low and high linguistic abilities. I also try to obtain a mix of other skills. For example, I may try to include at least one student with strong artistic or musical skills in each group.

2. **Mixed-gender grouping:** I attempt to have at least one boy and one girl in each group. Over the years, I have noticed that the small groups seem to stay on task more frequently, produce more, and have fewer social problems when composed this way than do single-sex groups.

3. **Roles emerge in groups:** Although cooperative learning experts often suggest assigning specific roles to group members, I have sometimes found this approach counterproductive. For example, Richard, whom I refer to in the introduction, might not have had an opportunity to express his musical talents had he been assigned to serve as scribe in his cooperative groups. I do assign roles, however, at the Interpersonal Center, where students are intentionally practicing social skills.

4. **One month timeframes:** While teachers select varying lengths of time for groups to stay together, I have found that starting new groups at the beginning of each month has proved most successful. One month is long enough for group members to get to know each other and to learn

to work well together; it is short enough that no one feels stuck in a particular group for too long. By working together for only four weeks at a time, students have an opportunity to get to know everyone in the class and to practice their collaborative skills with various individuals.

5. **Groups stay together during centers:** As students move through the learning centers, they usually stay with their assigned groups. This varied composition minimizes behavioral problems. I allow more flexibility with this rule as the year goes along: some students will move ahead of their groups briefly or stay behind to complete something as the situation requires.

Starting a Multiple Intelligences Program

Teachers frequently ask, "How do I get started? I like the idea of Multiple Intelligences, but I'm not sure where to begin." First of all, it is important to identify what the teacher is already doing that incorporates some of the intelligences into students' learning opportunities. (It is also important to acknowledge areas that one simply overlooks or avoids.) Next, teachers should realize that working with Multiple Intelligences affects more than instructional methods: it also influences how teachers perceive students, develop curriculum, and assess students' work. Interestingly, it also influences how teachers perceive themselves as teachers. Some suggestions for getting started follow:

1. **Create the environment:** One of the first steps in developing a differentiated classroom using MI is enhancing the physical environment so that it can accommodate multiple ways of learning. Some teachers replace student desks with tables for more space. Some simply rearrange the existing furniture so that there are spaces for small-group, whole-group, and individual learning. Some high school teachers plan units and lessons together and actually use each other's classrooms as needed, to take advantage of a drama stage or science lab.

   To begin my program I asked the school custodian to remove the individual desks from my classroom and to replace them with tables. The tables he found didn't match and were not in the best condition; however, simply having students seated at tables immediately changed my role as a teacher, giving me much more physical space than when the room was filled with more than thirty individual desks. Figure 1.1 shows how my classroom space is organized.

   In addition to changing the physical environment, the teacher must gather a variety of resources, as hands-on materials are needed to engage each of the intelligences. A list of suggested resources follows in the next section.

2. **Identify curriculum units:** In most schools curriculum is determined by state standards and district curricular scope and sequence. Some teachers teach thematically while others teach discrete disciplinary areas. However one approaches classroom curriculum, I like to create a thematic curriculum. I begin by identifying major themes in the curriculum. Next, I determine the important concepts and skills I plan to teach explicitly, and then I create individual lessons and assessment approaches based on the state standards. For example, a quarter-long theme I taught was Motion in Space and on Earth. This science unit addressed the structure of matter and the mechanics of objects, forces, and motion. One lesson was "What Are Asteroids and How Do They Move?" By identifying my curriculum's concepts and lessons, I can begin planning how to differentiate instruction by using Multiple Intelligences. Students learn about asteroids in various ways, again with an emphasis on reading and writing.

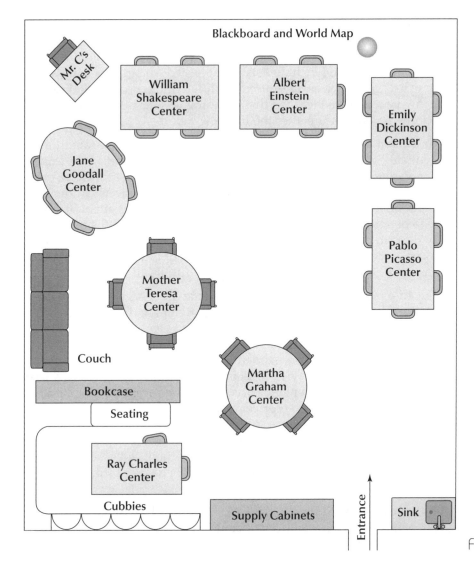

Blackboard and World Map

Mr. C's Desk

William Shakespeare Center

Albert Einstein Center

Emily Dickinson Center

Jane Goodall Center

Pablo Picasso Center

Mother Teresa Center

Couch

Martha Graham Center

Bookcase

Seating

Ray Charles Center

Cubbies

Supply Cabinets

Entrance

Sink

FIGURE 1.1

3. **Identify desired outcomes:** In addition to knowing what I want to teach and what input the students will receive, I also have to identify what output I expect from my students. I need to identify what students should know and do after they have studied the unit. One of the challenges inherent in differentiating instruction through Multiple Intelligences is finding diverse ways to teach content. During my first year of MI teaching, I dedicated most of my efforts to creating activities that engaged each intelligence in learning. Some of these activities were merely that—activities. They did not offer valuable learning experiences for students. I quickly realized that I needed to determine what was most valuable for students to know and do, based on their readiness, abilities of learning profiles. Beginning with a worthwhile outcome better determines how to teach in meaningful ways. Some of the differentiated outcomes I have worked with have included writing a research report, making a collage, conducting an interview, composing a three-part rhythm, and drawing a graph with X and Y coordinates.

4. **Plan MI instructional strategies:** MI teaching techniques present the desired content and provide students with practice in differentiated

ways. For example, students might learn the skill of organizing information visually while they are classifying plants and animals in their respective ecosystems. Because it takes a while to begin thinking of multiple ways to teach, I include lists of suggested MI strategies in Part III. These lists can serve as a resource for differentiated planning. From my own experience I learned that planning lessons in several modes becomes second nature after the first few months.

5. **Use varied assessment tools:** Just as any content can be taught in differentiated ways, it can also be assessed in differentiated ways. I use a wide variety of assessment tools in my classroom. These include portfolios, art work, songs, and videotapes of student projects. Students should be involved in the decision making about assessment. Before they are to be assessed, students should, in conjunction with the teacher, identify the criteria to be used to assess their work, as well as the rubric that will be applied. When students know ahead of time what the assessment consists of, they can make sure their work fulfills all criteria.

6. **Plan to extend each student's strengths:** Teachers should observe students while they are engaged in various activities and note which activities students find enjoyable, struggle with, or even try to avoid. In doing so, teachers can find ways to bridge student strengths to their areas of weakness. For example, one student of mine, Jason, found mechanical tasks pleasurable, while writing seemed impossible to him. I asked Jason to create a dictionary of engine parts. He did and went on to write a narrative explanation of how to replace oil in a car.

   Planning ways to enhance student strengths can be easily accomplished through offering independent projects, encouraging students to participate in enrichment activities—such as school clubs—or inviting experts into the classroom to work with small groups of students in apprenticeships.

7. **Share your ideas:** When you are planning to differentiate instruction with MI in your classroom, share your intentions, efforts, and questions with colleagues, administrators, parents and, most importantly, students, for feedback and refinement.

Resources for a Differentiated, Multiple Intelligences Learning Environment

There are basic resources that are useful for teaching and learning in a differentiated classroom. Many of these items are already present in most schools; they simply need to be made readily available for students to use. Teachers can share and circulate resources, and students can be asked to bring items from home.

What follows is a cursory list of suggested materials to engage all intelligences. It is not necessary to have all items in the classroom at any one time. What is important, however, is to have a variety of resources available and to provide numerous opportunities for students to work with them.

I have listed the MI resources in Figures 1.2–1.9. The first column identifies resources appropriate for teaching to each intelligence. The teacher can mark the second column with checks to track the items that the teacher currently has, and mark the third column with stars to designate those items that teacher might like to acquire. I accumulated most of my MI resources over the course of a couple years with small yearly grants that the district made available.

VERBAL–LINGUISTIC RESOURCES

Resources	Check if you already possess	Star if you would like to acquire
Reading materials		
trade books		
newspapers		
reference books		
encyclopedias		
dictionaries		
thesauruses		
a variety of magazines		
student-made books		
student-selected reading materials		
bulletin and message boards		
word mobiles		
sentence strips		
pocket charts		
materials for English language learners		
Writing materials		
paper, pens, pencils		
letter stencils		
notebooks		
computers		
desktop publishing software		
printers' bookmaking materials		

FIGURE 1.2

LOGICAL–MATHEMATICAL RESOURCES

Resources	Check if you already possess	Star if you would like to acquire
Math manipulatives		
objects to serve as counters		
pattern blocks		
Unifix® Cubes		
tangrams		
puzzles		
strategy games		
blocks		
Cuisenaire® Rods		
dice		
collections for sorting		
construction sets		
Measuring tools		
rulers		
protractors		
tape measures		
balance scales		
measuring cups		

FIGURE 1.3

KINESTHETIC RESOURCES

Resources	Check if you already possess	Star if you would like to acquire
Props for skits and movement		
streamers		
hats, scarves, capes		
costumes		
miscellaneous props: suitcase, umbrella, etc.		
Hands-on materials		
construction sets		
stacking blocks		
connecting blocks		
puppets		
tools		
building materials		
fabric and sewing materials		
puzzles		
board games		
craft supplies		

FIGURE 1.4

VISUAL–SPATIAL RESOURCES

Resources	Check if you already possess	Star if you would like to acquire
Art materials		
paints		
clay		
markers, crayons		
collage materials		
pastels, colored pencils		
stencils		
rubber stamps		
drafting supplies		
Visuals		
charts		
posters		
diagrams		
graphs		
puzzles		
art prints		
flash cards		
graphic software		
videotapes		
video equipment		

FIGURE 1.5

MUSICAL RESOURCES		
Resources	Check if you already possess	Star if you would like to acquire
Listening equipment		
CDs		
headphones		
recording equipment		
CD players		
music software		
Instruments		
keyboards		
rhythm sticks		
tambourines		
drums		
homemade instruments		
"soft" percussion: shakers, beanbags		
stringed instruments		

FIGURE 1.6

INTERPERSONAL RESOURCES

Resources	Check if you already possess	Star if you would like to acquire
tables (instead of desks) or other seating arrangements to facilitate small-group work		
group-oriented games and puzzles		
problems to solve cooperatively, such as learning materials with components that one group has to teach to another		
board games		
software programs for cooperative work		
autobiographies and biographies		
conflict-resolution procedures		
tutoring opportunities		
group projects		

FIGURE 1.7

INTRAPERSONAL RESOURCES

Resources	Check if you already possess	Star if you would like to acquire
a quiet place for students to work independently		
journals		
stories, books, news articles that provide illustrations of character development and personal identity		
independent projects		
personal collections or artifacts		
a bulletin board or other means to acknowledge students' strengths and contributions		

FIGURE 1.8

NATURALIST RESOURCES

Resources	Check if you already possess	Star if you would like to acquire
magnifying glasses or jeweler's loupes		
materials for pressing flowers or leaves		
scrapbooks		
microscopes		
books about plants, animals, bugs, birds, trees, etc.		
nature center		
egg cartons for collecting and sorting		
seeds, dirt, and paper cups or containers		
shells, rocks, feathers, etc.		

FIGURE 1.9

Preparing Students and Parents for Differentiated Instruction through Multiple Intelligences

Because the Theory of Multiple Intelligences is not necessarily familiar to either your students or their parents, you need to educate both groups about the many ways there are to be intelligent.

Part II begins with a story that serves as a parable of the Multiple Intelligences. This is a story I tell to introduce Gardner's work to teachers in my workshops. It is also a story I tell to students to help them understand that there are many ways to solve problems. After the story, you will find a simple description, written for students in grades four through twelve, of Gardner's theory.

Next, I include a sample letter to be sent home to parents at the beginning of the school year to explain an MI classroom program. You'll also find a student inventory that asks students to reflect on how they best like to learn. Lastly, you will find the book's first lesson plan—one on the Multiple Intelligences. It teaches students about the Multiple Intelligences by engaging all of their intelligences in learning.

24

Part II: Preparing
Students and
Parents for
Differentiated
Instruction through
Multiple
Intelligences

Part II Contents

"The Prince": A Parable for Multiple Intelligences

This story can be read aloud by the teacher or photocopied for students to read. It introduces students to the Theory of Multiple Intelligences. It is the story of a prince who sets out on a journey and encounters diverse challenges. To resolve these challenges, the prince must rely upon all his intelligences.

For the teacher or storyteller, there are some simple materials to gather beforehand. These include:

- One small bag of pennies (for use as gold coins)
- A small, flattened piece of clay and a short stick (about 3–4 inches)
- A rock
- A small balance scale
- Three balls or scarves for juggling (*a simple sleight-of-hand magic trick can be substituted for juggling, to illustrate the kinesthetic problem*)
- A pocket compass
- A small mirror
- A recorder or other small flute
- A bag of candy containing enough pieces for each student in the class
- A magnifying glass
- A bag to contain all of the above items

Italicized cues are given in the text to make use of the props. (Teachers who plan to photocopy the story might want to delete the instructions given in italics before giving the story to students.)

The Prince

There was once a young prince who lived long ago in a far-off land. As a child, the prince was taught not only how to ride, hunt, and swordfight but also how to write, read, count, and play music.

One day a sage—a wise old man—came into the kingdom and asked to see the queen and king. The sage told the king and queen of a precious gem that had been wrongfully taken from their kingdom many years before. He explained that they had to send their son, the prince, to reclaim it. The task would not be an easy one, for the gem was now in a distant land, and it was guarded by a terrible beast with the body of a lion, the claws of a vulture, and the head of a fire-breathing serpent.

The queen and king were reluctant to send their only son on such a dangerous journey. But the sage insisted and at last they relented. The prince prepared to leave and, as he did so, his parents each gave him a gift. His father gave him a small purse filled with gold coins and told his son to spend them wisely. *(Hold up small pouch with pennies.)* The prince's mother gave him a larger bag and explained that there were seven gifts inside. Each was to be used only in a time of great need. *(Hold up bag containing all items except the bag of coins and the rock.)*

The prince set out and traveled for many days and nights. One evening, as he was crossing a mountain pass, he was captured by a band of thieves. The thieves took the prince to their leader in a cave and ordered the youth to explain who he was and why he was traveling through their territory. The prince was also told that, if he could explain his mission well enough to their chief, he would be allowed to continue his journey; but also that, if he failed, he would have seen the sun rise for the last time.

Now before the chief, the prince began his story. The thieves began to laugh, and it was then the prince realized their chief was deaf and heard not a word he spoke. Wondering how best to proceed, the prince reached for the first time into the bag that his mother had given him *(reach into bag)* and pulled out a small clay tablet. Quickly he wrote, "Prince on a journey to reclaim stolen jewel," using the stick found in his bag. *(Write with stick on clay.)* The chief, impressed by the youth's ingenuity, sent him onward to continue his journey.

The prince traveled on. Some days later, he came to a great sea that he realized he must cross. There was only one ship in port, and it was skippered by a ruthless captain who wanted no passengers aboard. The prince persisted in his request for passage. At last the captain reached down and picked up a stone from the beach. *(Have the stone ready to pick up now.)* He told the prince that, if he could precisely

26

Part II: Preparing
Students and
Parents for
Differentiated
Instruction through
Multiple
Intelligences

match the weight of that stone in gold, he would give him passage across the sea. If he failed, he would have to wait for the next ship to come—which might be several months away.

For the second time, the prince reached into the bag of gifts his mother had given him. This time he pulled out a small balance scale. He placed the stone in one side and began to count gold coins from the purse his father had given him into the other. *(Balance the scale with the stone and pennies.)* The scale balanced and the captain, like the thieves before him, was impressed with the prince's wit. And so the prince was given passage.

After a long journey across the sea, the prince came to another kingdom, where he was graciously welcomed, for the people in this land had received few visitors from afar. They asked the prince to meet their king before passing through, The king was saddened by a turn of fortune. The townspeople hoped the prince might please their king with stories of his journey. Upon meeting the king, the prince saw that he was truly a forlorn man. Realizing the challenge before him, the prince reached for the third time into his bag and pulled out three balls. *(Pull out balls or scarves and begin to juggle.)* He began to juggle them, and the king, who had never before seen such a skill, was delighted. He, too, gave the youth his blessing and sent him on his way.

The prince traveled on for many days and, as he did, he began to hear stories of a great fortress with rich treasure inside. Tales were told of one great gem in particular. The prince knew this had to be the jewel that rightfully belonged to his people. As he continued on, he also began to hear tales of a frightful beast inside the fortress, and of many explorers who had entered but were never seen again.

At last, the day came when the prince stood before the great fortress. The walls seemed endless and stretched in either direction as far as the eye could see. He looked and looked but could find no entrance. While searching for a way to enter the fortress, the prince noticed an old woman struggling with a large bundle of kindling on the road. The prince rushed to help her. He carried the wood home for her and built a crackling fire.

In exchange for his generosity, the old woman not only told the boy where to find the entrance to the fortress, she also explained that, once inside, he would find a great labyrinth. She warned him that many before him had entered this maze, but that none had returned. If the youth were to survive, he had to follow the first passage he entered to the north, until he came to an opening to the east. He was then to wind through this passage until he came to an opening to the south. He must follow this passage until he came to one opening to the west, and so on, following this pattern until at last he would arrive at the very center.

Thanking the old woman, the prince returned to the fortress and found the entrance. Once inside, though, he lost all sense of direction. And so, for the fourth time, he reached into the bag his mother had

27

Part II: Preparing
Students and
Parents for
Differentiated
Instruction through
Multiple
Intelligences

given him and pulled out a small compass. *(Take out the compass.)* Using the compass, the prince followed the directions of the old woman, north-east-south-west, and so on, until at last he came to the center of the labyrinth.

There in the center of the maze lay a great mound of treasure. On top was one brilliant stone, which the prince recognized as the goal of his journey. But guarding the treasure was a creature more hideous than anything he had imagined. Its huge, red eyes glowed, it belched fire, and around the beast were scattered the remains of others who had preceded the prince.

The creature realized that someone was in the maze. It roared and began to rise. Realizing that his small sword would be of little use against this frightening beast, the prince reached into his bag and this time he pulled out a small, wooden flute. Quickly he began to play an old lullaby that his nursemaid had sung to him as a child. *(Play simple, soft melody on flute.)* The beast paused and listened to the melody. As the prince continued to play, the beast, lulled by the music, slowed, stopped, and at last lay down and fell asleep. Continuing to play, the prince crept past the horrible creature, picked up the gem—the birthright of his land—and retraced his steps out of the labyrinth.

On his homeward journey, the prince's reputation preceded him. He was called this way and that to help a traveler in distress or to aid a troubled village. One evening, as he traveled down a desolate road, he realized that he had wandered so far from his original path that he was entirely lost. It was then that he came upon a group of vagabonds, travelers like himself, but clearly impoverished and starving. The prince knew that they could help him. Before he could ask them for any help, though, he had to do something for them first. And so, reaching for the sixth time into his bag, he pulled out a smaller bag and handed it to one of the travelers, who found something wonderful inside. *(Hand bag of candy to someone in the audience.)* He in turn passed the bag along to his companions, and each of them found something of pleasure.

The travelers and the prince quickly became friends. They not only directed the prince toward his homeland but also agreed to accompany him. And so they traveled on together until the day the prince saw the hills of his own kingdom. But, alas, one final obstacle loomed before him, for a great fissure had opened in the earth and hot lava poured forth, spreading as far as could be seen. There was nothing the prince feared more than the heat and steam of the lava. Despaired, he sat down and wondered how he could have traveled so far only to fail.

As he sat, one of his companions approached and told the prince about a way to cross the lava. But no one could tell the prince what it was. Rather, he had to discover it for himself. And so, for the seventh time, he reached into the bag that his mother had given him and pulled out a small mirror. Looking into the mirror and seeing his own reflection, the prince realized that only through his own courage and determination could he overcome this final challenge.

28

Part II: Preparing
Students and
Parents for
Differentiated
Instruction through
Multiple
Intelligences

With new resolve, the prince arose and picked up his bag. Without looking down at the hot lava, he walked unharmed to the other side, instead gazing into the distance at his homeland.

And so the prince returned home and was welcomed as a great hero. In time he, too, became king and ruled wisely and fairly. And in the years and generations that followed, he was remembered not only for his kindness but for his ability to solve many problems in many ways.

That's the end of the story about the prince. However, there is a sequel to the story. After serving as king for many years, in his old age, he turned the throne over to his own son. In his last years, he decided to write a book about all of his travels, including details about the plants and animals of all the lands through which he had passed. The book was read for years to come and, in the end, the prince was remembered not only for being a great king and problem solver, but also for being a great naturalist. *(Take out magnifying glass.)*

After sharing this story, the teacher might want to explain Gardner's Theory of Multiple Intelligences and have the class relate the prince's challenges to each intelligence.

Teaching Parents and Students about Differentiated Instruction and the Multiple Intelligences

Sometimes it is useful to have a brief description of the Theory of Multiple Intelligences for students to read and to send home to parents. Teachers might want to provide the following explanation to students as part of a lesson on Multiple Intelligences. Sending the explanation home to parents will help them understand how their students are learning and what they mean when they use terms like *kinesthetic*, *intrapersonal*, and *Multiple Intelligences*. At the end of the description I suggest some questions for students and their parents to discuss.

The Theory of Multiple Intelligences: An Explanation for Students and Parents

As a teacher, I believe that there are many strengths that students possess. Not all individuals are smart in the same ways. Students each have their own talents that they use and express differently from one another. Many of my ideas about how both children and adults learn are based on the Theory of Multiple Intelligences developed by a Harvard psychologist named Howard Gardner. Gardner, too, believes that there are multiple ways that people can be smart. An explanation of the Theory of Multiple Intelligences follows, as do more about the ideas that influence how I differentiate instruction for my students. First, I will begin by defining several terms:

- A *theory* attempts to explain how and why certain things happen. A simple example of a theory is "the domino theory" that suggests if one event occurs it will lead to another.

- *Multiple* means "many."

- *Intelligence* is the ability to learn, to solve problems, and to become smarter.

- A *psychologist* is a scientist who studies how people think and act. Howard Gardner is a psychologist at Harvard University who created a new theory of intelligence.

- The *Theory of Multiple Intelligences* says that there are many ways in which people can learn, solve problems, and be smart. The Theory of Multiple Intelligences was created by psychologist Howard Gardner. In his Theory of Multiple Intelligences, Gardner says that there are at least eight kinds of human intelligence and that people can be smart in one or more ways. Howard Gardner describes these intelligences as follows:

  1. **Linguistic intelligence** is the ability to think in words and use language to express ideas. Authors, poets, speakers, and newscasters are strong examples of people with linguistic intelligence.

  2. **Logical–mathematical intelligence** is the ability to calculate, measure, use logic, and solve math and science problems. Scientists, mathematicians, accountants, and detectives rely on this intelligence.

  3. **Bodily–kinesthetic intelligence** is the ability to use bodies and hands with great skill. Dancers, athletes, surgeons, jugglers, and craftspeople use this intelligence in their work.

  4. **Visual–spatial intelligence** is the ability to think in pictures and to see and create images or designs with shape, color, and size. Painters, architects, sculptors, sailors, and pilots exhibit this intelligence.

  5. **Musical intelligence** is the ability to hear and use pitch, rhythm, and tone. Singers, musicians, composers, and skilled listeners demonstrate this intelligence.

  6. **Interpersonal intelligence** is the ability to understand and interact with other people in a variety of ways. Teachers, coaches, ministers, actors, social workers, and politicians all use this intelligence.

  7. **Intrapersonal intelligence** is the ability to understand your feelings and who you are in the world. Philosophers, psychologists, and playwrights use this intelligence.

  8. **Naturalist intelligence** is the ability to see patterns in the natural world: plant growth, animal behavior, rocks, clouds, and so forth. Biologists, veterinarians, rock collectors, and environmentalists use this intelligence.

Dr. Gardner suggests there may be even more intelligences. For example, he theorizes about an existential intelligence, one which would have to do with religion or spirituality. Some day there might be many more forms of intelligence identified.

Everyone possesses all the intelligences. However, some of us use more of one, others more of another. The intelligences emerge at different ages: even if a particular intelligence is not prominent in a person as a child, that

30

Part II: Preparing
Students and
Parents for
Differentiated
Instruction through
Multiple
Intelligences

person may actually become more intelligent in that area later in life. Any of these intelligences can be developed through practice and effort.

The important things to remember are that everyone has different abilities and that everyone learns and thinks in unique ways. In my classroom, I like to make sure that students have opportunities to learn in many ways so that they can optimize their strengths and also bolster the areas in which they are more challenged. Some helpful questions for parents and MI students to discuss follow:

What are some of your favorite activities?

What intelligences do you use in your favorite activities?

What intelligences do you think are your strongest?

How have you developed these intelligences?

What role has school played in developing your intelligences?

What role have your life experiences played in developing your intelligences?

How do you use your intelligences in daily life?

Which intelligences would you like to develop more fully? Why? How would you use these intelligences?

How can schools do a better job of helping students use all their intelligences in learning?

A Letter to Parents

I have found it helpful to send a letter home to parents explaining what I am doing in my classroom and why. This letter describes my classroom and would accompany the explanation above. I invariably receive letters from parents in response, expressing their appreciation for my letter and interest in MI. I have never received a negative response (and keep my fingers crossed!).

```
Dear parents,

With a new school year beginning, I would like to
inform you about how I plan to teach your children
this year. Because all students have their own inter-
ests and abilities, I approach the school year as an
adventure with new challenges. Some of those chal-
lenges are to help students individually discover how
they learn best, how to optimize their individual tal-
ents, and how to help them use their strengths to
overcome their weaknesses. I organize my classroom to
address these challenges.

    The way I organize my classroom is unique in that
it allows students to work at learning centers each
```

morning. Students move from center to center in small groups, and at each center they learn the day's lesson in a different way. The ways in which they learn are based on a theory developed by Harvard psychologist Howard Gardner. In his book, *Frames of Mind: The Theory of Multiple Intelligences*, Gardner says that everyone's mind is unique and that we all learn best in different ways.

I have enclosed a fact sheet on Howard Gardner's Theory of Multiple Intelligences. The students will be reading this at one of the learning centers during the first week of school. As you will see, the students in my classroom learn not only through reading, writing, and math, but also through making and listening to music, making and appreciating art, building, moving, interacting with each other, thinking, and reflecting.

In addition to their work at the centers, the students have independent projects that they must work on each month. These research projects are of the students' choice and require three to four weeks to prepare. When students have completed their research, they must teach the rest of the class about what they have learned, using charts and diagrams, skits, music, stories, graphs, time lines, models, songs, videotapes, problems for the class to solve, and puzzles. The learning centers in my classroom teach students academic content, as well as the skills to learn in these different ways. The independent projects deepen content knowledge and sharpen learning skills while letting students pursue the topics that interest them most. Project work is exciting and highly motivating for the students. I encourage you to become involved in working with your students on the research and preparation of their projects.

Finally, I am always looking for adults who are intelligent in a variety of ways to work with students in the classroom. Do you play an instrument? Are you a craftsperson? Do you know a lot about a particular topic? Or do you just love your work? Please let me know, because I would like to invite you to come in and share your talents or interests with the class. In fact, I invite you to come in just to visit, ask questions, and learn more about what we are doing. I look forward to working with both you and your student this year.

Sincerely yours,

Part II: Preparing
Students and
Parents for
Differentiated
Instruction through
Multiple
Intelligences

Student Self-Reflection Inventory

Your Current Learning Preferences

Name: _____

1. What is your favorite subject at school? _____

2. What do you like to spend your time at home doing?
_____

3. How do you like to learn about things (reading, drawing, acting things out, etc.) _____

4. Check all of the things you think you are good at:
_____ reading
_____ discussing
_____ journal writing, poetry, other kinds of writing
_____ music (singing, rhythm, listening, playing instruments)
_____ art (drawing, painting, sculpting, collage, etc.)
_____ math (calculating, solving story problems, measuring, etc.)
_____ movement activities (acting, dancing, juggling, etc.)
_____ building activities (constructing things)
_____ working with others
_____ working or playing with animals
_____ working alone and thinking about things
_____ doing things in nature

5. List other things you think you do well that are not listed above:
_____

6. What do you think is your strongest intelligence? Check one:
linguistic _____   mathematical _____
kinesthetic _____   visual _____
musical _____   interpersonal _____
intrapersonal _____   naturalist _____

7. What would you like to be better at? _____

8. What do you think you are getting better at? _____

9. What subjects would you like to learn more about? _____

10. What other thoughts or suggestions do you have to make school— or this class—more interesting? _____

After students have been introduced to the Theory of Multiple Intelligences, teachers might consider having them respond to this inventory. It asks students to reflect on their strengths, and it provides teachers with useful information on how students like to learn and how they perceive their own abilities.

If educators administer this inventory before they begin teaching, it will provide them with general information to measure how students change throughout the course of the year.

In my own classroom, after administering the inventory at the beginning of the school year, I find that most students prefer to learn in two to four ways. As they have opportunities to learn in all eight intelligences over the course of the year, their learning preferences increase.

Administering this inventory at the beginning of the year, and once or twice throughout the year, helps teachers determine how students' learning preferences and perceptions of their own talents have changed. Nonetheless, this is not necessarily a valid or reliable instrument, nor are others' inventories or surveys like it. They simply provide different perspectives on students in the classroom.

Lesson 1: A Differentiated Eight-Part Lesson on Multiple Intelligences

This is the first differentiated lesson plan in this book. It is offered here to introduce students to Multiple Intelligences. The suggested activities can be presented in any order and can be taught with the whole class or at learning centers. I have written the directions for each of the centers. If they so desire, teachers may simply photocopy the activities and give them to their students.

Subject Areas: science, health

Main Concept: Human intelligence is multi-faceted

Principle Taught: Individuals have unique cognitive profiles

Unit: Our Bodies, Our Brains, Our Abilities

Grade Level: 3–12

Materials Needed

Teachers should photocopy and make available to students:

1. "The Theory of Multiple Intelligences: an Explanation for Students and Parents" for the linguistic activity

2. Logical–mathematical story problem for all students

3. One copy of each fact sheet about the eight famous people for the interpersonal activity

4. One copy of the intrapersonal questions for each student

5. One blank copy of the pie chart for the visual–spatial activity for each student

6. Enough simple musical instruments for students to use in small groups

Linguistic Activity

Students should start by reading "The Theory of Multiple Intelligences: an Explanation for Students and Parents." After having read the information, students can discuss what it means to be smart, which intelligences they think are their strongest, and whom they know who is smart in one or more of the intelligences.

34

Part II: Preparing
Students and
Parents for
Differentiated
Instruction through
Multiple
Intelligences

Logical–Mathematical Activity

Students can try solving the following problem:

Gabriel, Daniel, Gracie, Maria, Li, Kumar, Chandra, and Jamal are at Jamal's house, trying to solve a problem their teacher has assigned for homework. Each of the students is particularly talented in one form of intelligence.

Gabriel is the most physically active and likes to move around while solving the problem. Neither Maria nor Li like to be alone. Gracie asks Jamal to turn the stereo off. Daniel doesn't like solving problems unless he can use some kind of formula. Kumar brought all his art supplies. Li brought a pile of books. Jamal is busy organizing the whole group. Chandra ignores everyone and spends the afternoon rearranging her collection of seashells.

Which student relies upon which intelligence? List their individual strengths below:

Gabriel _____   Gracie _____

Daniel _____   Li _____

Jamal _____   Kumar _____

Maria _____   Chandra _____

Kinesthetic Activity

In small groups students brainstorm a list of jobs that require physical skills, such as carpenter or surgeon. Students should then identify two of these jobs and create brief, silent pantomimes that show the activities people perform in the selected jobs. Students in other groups guess what jobs the groups are portraying.

Visual–Spatial Activity

Students make a pie chart of their intelligences, divide their circles into eight sections. The size of each section represents how talented the students each perceive themselves in that intelligence.

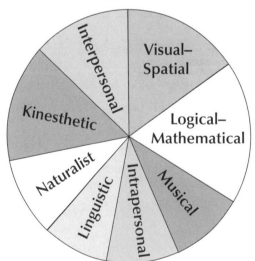

For example, a student who likes to read, write, and talk might make a large section for linguistic intelligence, and a small section for musical intelligence if that student does not sing, play instruments, or listen to music very much.

Musical Activity

Using the instruments provided, students create a rhythm to accompany the following lyrics:

> Multiple Intelligences are really cool.
> It means that nobody is a fool.
> Everyone can sing his or her own praise,
> Because we are smart in so many ways.

Interpersonal Activity

Students break into small groups and ask one person in each group to read aloud a fact sheet about a famous person who demonstrates a particular intelligence. After the fact sheet has been read, students discuss:

■ Which intelligence this person demonstrated,

■ How this person expressed his or her intelligence,

■ Why this person is famous, and

■ Other people they know who possess similar strengths.

Profiles of Intelligence Exemplars

William Shakespeare

William Shakespeare was an English writer who lived four hundred years ago. He wrote poems and plays and is considered the greatest dramatist (a person who writes plays) and the greatest English language poet who ever lived. He is still the most popular author in the world. His plays have been performed thousands of times in countries around the world.

Some of his most famous plays are *Richard III, Romeo and Juliet, Macbeth, Hamlet,* and *A Midsummer Night's Dream.* He wrote three kinds of plays: comedies, tragedies, and histories. *A Midsummer Night's Dream* is a comedy, *Macbeth* is a tragedy, and *Richard III* is a historical play.

The reason Shakespeare is so famous is he understood people and their life experiences. The characters in his plays appeal to all kinds of audiences because they address topics that people deal with in their daily lives—jealousy, struggle for power, and love.

Albert Einstein

Albert Einstein was one of the greatest scientists who ever lived. He studied time, space, mass, motion, and gravity. He is famous for his equation $E = mc^2$ (Energy equals mass time the speed of light squared), which suggests that matter and energy two different forms of the same thing. Understanding this equation made it possible for scientists to develop atomic energy and the atomic bomb.

Einstein developed his theories not only through mathematical calculations but also through deep, reflective thinking. He was very interested in philosophy, music, and politics. He believed strongly in world peace, even though his ideas led to the development of the atomic bomb.

Before Einstein, scientists believed that light was a kind of wave. Einstein suggested that light could be thought of as a tiny stream of particles called *quanta.* This discovery led to the invention of movies and television.

36

Part II: Preparing
Students and
Parents for
Differentiated
Instruction through
Multiple
Intelligences

One of Einstein's most famous discoveries is the theory of relativity, which is about time and space. He determined that, if a space traveler were to leave Earth and travel far out into space, when he returned he would be younger than if he had remained on Earth.

Martha Graham

Martha Graham was an American dancer and choreographer (someone who creates dances). She founded modern dance and used her entire body to express her inner feelings and thoughts in dance. Many of her dances were not considered graceful because feelings like anger, fear, and hatred called for rough and jagged motions. During the 1930s, 1940s, and 1950s, Martha Graham's dances shocked audiences with their unique style. Yet, because of the dances she created, people began to look at this art form in new ways.

Graham began dancing as a young girl in the early 1900s and continued to dance for over eighty years. Many of her dances described myths, the experiences of women, and the experiences of people from rural America and diverse cultures. She said that dance made our inner feelings visible.

Pablo Picasso

Picasso was the most famous painter of the twentieth century. He created new styles of art and often, when one style became accepted, Picasso would create an entirely new form. He responded to the changing conditions in the world during the twentieth century and to his own changing feelings. His art reflected these transformations.

Picasso's paintings seemed to be filled with strange and distorted images, ones that might be glimpsed in nightmares. In using these images, he seemed to be trying to connect the viewer with his or her own inner thoughts and feelings. Much of Picasso's art was influenced by the art of his home country of Spain during the Spanish Civil War.

One of his earliest stages as a painter is called the Blue Period because many of his paintings at that time included a great deal of blue. Next, Picasso switched to warm colors and expressed a variety of moods in his paintings. He went through a stage of painting circus scenes and then massive figures. Next, his paintings became so jagged and distorted that it was difficult to identify who or what was in the paintings. In a later stage, Picasso began to include newspaper clippings, words, and pieces of debris in his work. In addition to his paintings, Picasso is also famous for his sculptures, ceramics, and drawings.

Ray Charles

Ray Charles was a black American singer and songwriter. He rose to popularity in the 1950s as a jazz singer.

Charles became blind at the age of six. He played the piano and sang with emotion and enthusiasm. His songs range from rock to blues. "I Got A Woman" was the hit song that propelled him to the forefront of American music. "What I Say" and "Georgia on My Mind" are two other well known Charles hits.

Early in his career he sang with several bands, but Charles mostly preferred to do solo performances. He influenced musicians around the world.

Mother Teresa

Mother Teresa was a Roman Catholic nun who lived in India and worked with the poor, starving, and sick people of Calcutta. Mother Teresa was born in Yugoslavia and became a nun at the age of eighteen. In 1948 she left her convent and went to Calcutta, one of the poorest cities in the world. She began a religious order in India and oversaw it for more than fifty years, providing hospitals, schools, shelters, orphanages, and youth centers for people who were hungry, sick, or dying. Here she was inspired to attend to those in greatest need. Her work branched out to over fifty cities in India and to over thirty countries around the world.

Her work earned her numerous awards and prizes. In 1979 she received the Nobel Peace Prize for her work helping the poor. This prize is generally given to world leaders and is considered the highest humanitarian award in the world.

Emily Dickinson

Emily Dickinson was a great American poet who lived in the late 1800s. She is still considered one of the finest poets to write in the English language.

She lived most of her life secluded in her family home in Massachusetts. She never married and had very few friends. She spent her time alone, pondering her deepest feelings, and writing about them. Those who have studied her work suggest that, because she spent so much time examining her feelings, she was able to write about them in unique ways.

Her poems are generally short and have no titles. Most of them are sad and deal with loneliness, anxiety, and death. She also wrote about the soul, God, and immortality. Dickinson wrote over 1,700 poems, but only seven of them were published during her lifetime, and those seven without her permission. She wrote secretly; her sister discovered her work after the poet died.

Jane Goodall

Jane Goodall is one of the world's most famous scientists. For many years she lived with wild chimpanzees in Africa and changed how we think about both chimps and ourselves. Her research continues to this day and is the longest field study of any group of animals in the wild. Goodall also travels around the world, teaching other people about chimpanzees and their environment.

She teaches about how chimpanzees are humankind's closest relatives in the animal kingdom. Her work shows that chimpanzees are highly intelligent, very sociable, and found only in Africa. They share over 98 percent of their genetic material with humans. They communicate and express many of the same emotions that humans do. Sadly, though, Jane Goodall's work has also shown that, while the world's human population continues to grow, its chimpanzee population is in decline.

Intrapersonal Activity

Now that students have been introduced to the idea of Multiple Intelligences, they are ready to analyze their individual strengths and abilities. Students

38

Part II: Preparing
Students and
Parents for
Differentiated
Instruction through
Multiple
Intelligences

may think silently for a few minutes and then with their group members discuss one of more of the following prompts:

What do you perceive as your strongest area of intelligence?

How did you develop this ability?

How could you improve your expertise in this area?

In what new way could you use your ability?

What new intelligence would you like to develop?

Naturalist Activity

Students group the following animals according to shared characteristics. Students should pay attention to the kind of thinking they use to sort the animals.

Bear	Moose	Trout	Walrus
Spider	Squirrel	Otter	Daffodil
Fern	Sheep	Apple tree	Oak tree
Shark	Marigold	Mosquito	Badger
Humpback whale	Eagle	Seal	Shark
Honeybee	Porpoise	Beaver	Elephant
Salmon	Cow	Deer	Dandelion
Fox	Gopher	Goat	Leopard
Bluebird	Dolphin	Tulip	Dragonfly
Beetle	Pine tree	Cedar tree	Tuna
Maple tree	Pig	Bass	Giraffe
Ladybug	Mink	Firefly	Butterfly

Assessment

To show their understanding of the Theory of Multiple Intelligences, students prepare a demonstration about MI for their class. They can work independently, or with one or two other students. Their demonstration should include one or more of the following elements:

1. A short skit or interview demonstrating that different people are smart in at least eight different ways

2. A poster with labels and pictures of each of the eight intelligences, the pictures drawn or cut from magazines

3. A brief story or description of the theory, using famous people whom the other students will recognize

4. A questionnaire that students can use to identify their own areas of intelligence

5. A song about MI that mentions all eight intelligences and how people can be smart in these ways

The following rubric can be used to evaluate the effectiveness of students' demonstrations.

A MULTIPLE INTELLIGENCES ASSESSMENT RUBRIC

POSSIBLE SCORES			
	Excellent	**Sufficient**	**Needs Improvement**
CRITERIA			
Presented in several intelligences			
Showed understanding of the eight intelligences			
Was clear and easy to understand			
Addressed specific state standards			

Part III

Preparing for
Differentiation with MI

Many teachers are interested in differentiating instruction through Multiple Intelligences. Yet it is human nature to teach from areas of strength and to avoid modes that are uncomfortable.

This section of the handbook asks teachers to reflect on their current modes of instruction and to consider the support they might need to teach in additional modes. I attempt to provide support for Multiple Intelligences–based pedagogy by offering a variety of instructional strategies for each intelligence. Teachers may want to review each list by checking off strategies currently used and starring those that could be easily incorporated into daily teaching. For each intelligence I also describe one instructional strategy in greater depth. At the end of this section teachers will find two handouts for students—one on spelling and one on multiplication—that integrate all eight intelligences into these two essential skill areas.

Part III Contents

- Sample Visual–Spatial Activity: Student-Made Cards
- Musical Strategies to Differentiate
  - Sample Musical Activity: Curriculum Songs
- Interpersonal Strategies to Differentiate
  - Sample Interpersonal Activity: Mix-and-Match Grouping
- Intrapersonal Strategies to Differentiate
  - Sample Intrapersonal Activity: Student Options
- Naturalist Strategies to Differentiate
  - Sample Naturalist Activity: Creating a Class Garden
- Differentiating Spelling Using MI
- Differentiating Multiplication Using MI

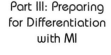

Teacher Self-Reflection Inventory

The inventory on page 42 is offered to help teachers reflect on how they currently teach. After taking the inventory, teachers should review it to see which intelligences they normally overlook in their instruction. They may want to focus on any neglected areas by incorporating instructional strategies suggested in the following pages of this handbook.

Linguistic Strategies to Differentiate

1. For five minutes students do "quick writes" reacting to lesson information.

2. Students tell stories of how they apply ideas from any discipline to their lives outside of school.

3. To practice accuracy in communication, pairs of students listen to each other give directions for an assignment.

4. To learn vocabulary for any topic, students create crossword puzzles.

5. Students debate diverse perspectives on any issue.

6. Students describe in writing the most meaningful content they have studied.

7. In small groups students give impromptu, one-minute presentations to group members on topics (of teacher's choice) drawn from recent lessons.

8. When reading classroom material, students review each page by creating keywords or phrases for the content of that page.

9. Students create short talk-show programs for which they pose as junior experts on classroom topics.

10. Using a word that represents a major concept, such as *interdependence*, students write a phrase that begins with each letter of the word to explain its meaning.

Sample Linguistic Activity: Journal Writing

Journals can be integrated into any subject area, and students can maintain journals for numerous purposes: to explain lesson content or problem-solving approaches, to express feelings about the content studied, to

Teacher Self-Reflection Inventory

My primary intelligence strengths are:

1. _____

2. _____

3. _____

The content I teach typically engages the following intelligences (Note whether there is any correlation with primary intelligence strengths listed above. If so, why? If not, why not?):

1. _____

2. _____

3. _____

4. _____

5. _____

The intelligences I typically teach through include:

1. _____

2. _____

3. _____

Examples of each intelligence I typically teach through are:

1. _____

2. _____

3. _____

One or more intelligences I usually overlook are:

1. _____

2. _____

The reason for such oversight is:

_____

_____

I would be willing to teach through the intelligence if:

_____

_____

Resources for doing so would include:

_____

_____

raise questions about what they don't understand, or to express concerns directly to the teacher. Before assigning journals, teachers should find out whether students are writing them in other classes. Several types of journals are described here to add variety to this worthwhile linguistic strategy:

Learning Logs

In learning logs students record the key concepts, supporting details, or problem-solving processes in their curriculum unit. They can be written in daily, weekly, or on occasion.

Personal Journals

In personal journals students determine the form and content of their own entries. They record their thoughts and feelings, much like they would in a diary. Some students might choose to write stories or poetry, or about their dreams, fears, or wishes. Some teachers request that students write in personal journals on a daily basis.

Notebook Journals

Leonardo da Vinci recorded his ideas in notebook journals. Such journals evolve from the interests of the students and take many forms, such as visual sketchbooks or statistical charting. Notebook journals are used on a spontaneous basis.

Dialogue Journals

Dialogue journals are generally shared with the teacher or other students. The student begins a story or narrative, and the teacher or a classmate responds. The response can be a personal comment or a continuation of the story. While this is time-consuming for teachers, it is motivating for students. Students usually write in dialogue journals on scheduled days of the week.

Simulation Journals

In simulation journals the student assumes the role of another person: an author, historical figure, scientist, imaginary character, animal, or inanimate object. These journals are used to help students understand diverse perspectives and are often assigned at irregular intervals.

Reading Journals

These journals record students' understanding, interpretation, critique, and analysis of their readings. Students write in them during and upon completion of assigned readings.

Class Journals

Everyone in the classroom contributes to class journals. A single journal is maintained on a podium or table for students, teachers, and guests to write entries on specified or spontaneous topics. These journals motivate students to read and write.

Logical–Mathematical Strategies to Differentiate

1. When given a problem, students plan strategies for ways to solve the problem before attempting its resolution.

2. Students are asked to discern patterns or relationships in the content of a lesson.

3. When offering solutions to any problem, students must provide a logical, rational support for their answers.

4. Students create or identify categories for sorting diverse data.

5. To extend classroom learning, students conduct surveys and analyze data on topics that they or the teacher have selected.

6. Working in pairs, students make up story problems involving the content of lesson.

7. Students engage in discussions that include higher-level thinking skills, such as comparing and contrasting, providing cause-and-effect answers, analyzing, hypothesizing, and synthesizing information.

8. As an independent or small-group project, students employ the scientific method to answer a question they have about a class topic.

9. Students study units focused on themes in math and science, such as probability, symmetry, randomness, and chaos.

10. Students use a variety of organizers to enhance logical thinking, such as outline charts, Venn diagrams, flow charts, and webs.

Sample Logical–Mathematical Activity: A Deductive Reasoning Game

Nearly everyone is familiar with the Jeopardy!™ game show, in which contestants must determine the appropriate question for each answer given. The same process can be used effectively in the classroom with any subject area. Jeopardy is a naturally differentiated game usually played with five tiers or five levels of difficulty. It lends itself well to the differentiated classroom. Teachers can create the questions but I like to have students generate them. They are more encouraged to play when they have a chance of selecting one of their own questions.

For years, I played classroom Jeopardy with a pocket chart, but now there are numerous digital versions of Jeopardy available online. Some are free, some are nicely produced with buzzers and other extras. The most basic ones are just PowerPoint documents. You can create your own template and or download one, then make multiple versions of it for different subjects or different units.

The "answers" may be relatively simple: Subject: Geography; Category: Continents for 100; Question: What is the coldest continent? Or they can be more complex: Subject: Cell Biology; Category: Mitosis; Question for 400: What is the sequential differentiation and segregation of replicated chromosomes in a cell nucleus that precedes complete cell division? Or they can involve higher level thinking skills: Subject: Environmental Science; Category: *The Energy Crisis*; Question for 300: What has the overuse of earth's energy sources and the increased demand for power created?

Kinesthetic Strategies to Differentiate

1. Students role-play any process such as photosynthesis, making a bill into a law, solving a quadratic equation, or the earth's orbit around the sun.

2. Working with small blocks, toothpicks, Legos®, or Popsicle® sticks, students build models of molecular chains, famous bridges, or towns in history or literature.

3. Teachers provide quick exercise breaks with simple calisthenics, tai chi or yoga, an active game of Simon Says, or even a jog around the playground.

4. In small groups students create large floor games that reinforce important concepts being studied.

5. Small groups of students represent countries with different resources to trade, or pioneers addressing the challenges of the frontier.

6. Teachers create scavenger hunts for students to gather information on a particular topic.

7. Regardless of the content, teachers may provide manipulatives for students to use to solve math problems, create patterns for art work, build replicas of cells or systems, or make storyboards as starting points for writing activities.

8. To extend classroom learning into the community, students go on field trips.

9. Students learn physical skills like juggling, dancing, balancing, rope jumping, climbing, hula hooping, bowling, throwing, catching, or working with tools.

10. Students pantomime what they have learned from a day's lesson.

Sample Kinesthetic Activity: Paper Plates

This is a simple, active game that is useful to review any topic. To prepare the game, the teacher obtains paper plates. Second, the teacher identifies the topic of focus and writes between five and ten pertinent questions with one-word answers. Third, the teacher writes the answers to these questions on the plates, with between three and five plates having the same answer. This format allows any number of students to play.

After scattering the plates, answer side up, around the room, the teacher explains to students that they will hear a question and must then find the paper plate that correctly answers that question. When they locate it, they must put a finger or toe on the plate as quickly as possible. When every student has found a correct answer-plate, the teacher reads another question, and off students go again.

There are two simple rules for playing games: students cannot touch anyone else (challenging when several students head for the same plate); students cannot make any noise (otherwise, they cannot hear the questions being read).

Four examples of paper plate games are shown here:

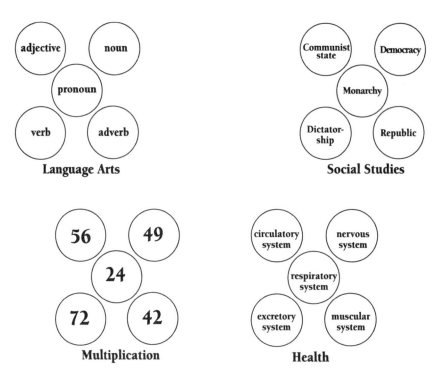

Language Arts

Social Studies

Multiplication

Health

Visual–Spatial Strategies to Differentiate

1. Students close their eyes and imagine themselves performing well on a test, speaking in front of the class, or successfully resolving a conflict.

2. Students create a pictorial representation of what they have learned from a unit of study, such as a chart, drawing, or mindmap.

3. Working independently or with a partner, students create a visual collage to display facts, concepts, and questions they have about a recent unit of study.

4. With access to computer graphics and page-layout programs, students illustrate their lessons.

5. Students diagram the structures of interconnected systems, such as body systems, economic systems, political systems, school systems, or food chains.

6. To communicate their understanding of a topic, students create flow charts, bar graphs, or pie charts.

7. Working in small groups, students create projects with video or photographs.

8. To work with three-dimensional activities, students design costumes or sets for literature or social studies; tools or experiments for science; and manipulative or new classroom or building designs for math.

9. Students create mobiles or design bulletin boards.

10. To demonstrate their understanding of a topic, students use color, shape, or rebus-type images in their papers.

Sample Visual–Spatial Activity: Student-Made Cards

Nearly anything can be learned or reviewed with student-made cards. Students can be creative in making these flash cards by decorating them with colors, shapes, and designs.

Cards can also be used to make simple games. Rummy, Go Fish, or Old Maid can be adapted to any subject area. The teacher simply needs to cut up card stock, construction paper, or note cards and plan the game according to the subject area. Students mark and illustrate the cards. A rubber stamp gives the cards uniformity on one side. Laminating them will make them durable.

Commercially produced games about authors, artists, scientists, explorers, and inventors are available through educational-materials catalogues and supply houses. However, the best ones are those that teachers or students make.

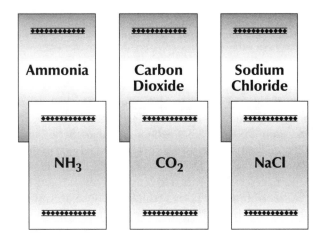

Musical Strategies to Differentiate

1. Teachers play background music to relax students or to focus their attention at various times of the day.

2. To review information, students compose curriculum songs, replacing the words to well-known songs with content-related lyrics.

3. Students make their own rhythm instruments for use with curriculum songs or recitations of arithmetic facts, spelling words, or sets of rules or facts.

4. Students select a song and explain how its lyrics relate to a lesson's content.

5. Students with access to musical software can add rhythmic accompaniment to multimedia reports and presentations.

6. Students select appropriate background music for book reports or other oral presentations.

7. To demonstrate patterns in mathematics, nature, and the visual arts, students use musical selections that are patterned and repetitive.

8. To become more familiar with a subject area, students listen to and analyze pre-recorded songs about that subject area.

9. Students analyze music to understand concepts like relationships between parts and wholes, fractions, repeating patterns, timing, and harmony.

10. Students use musical vocabulary as metaphors, such as crescendo for the climax of a short story, two-part harmony for interpersonal relations, or cadence for physical exercise.

Sample Musical Activity: Curriculum Songs

In addition to enhancing classroom ambiance, it is important to include music in the curriculum. Tapes with songs in the content areas are available through educational-materials catalogues for nearly any subject. Even more effective are teacher-made and student-made songs about topics being studied. Here is an example of a song about environmental pollution, composed by a group of third graders after a lesson on the ozone layer. It is sung to the tune of "Jingle Bells."

Jingle bells, garbage smells,
Diapers in the dump.
Styrofoam and CFCs,
They make me scream and jump. Oh

Jingle bells, garbage smells,
Pollution is a drag.
Toxic wastes from factories
Make me want to gag.

Students can be organized in small groups to write an entire song or to contribute a stanza to a class song. Students should be directed to select a song with a familiar tune. The teacher can also specify expectations, such as including ten concepts from a recent unit of study or including questions that the class still wants answered about a topic. Once students have written their songs, they should have opportunities to sing and teach them to the whole class.

A list of familiar songs follows. These all have simple and recognizable rhythms which can be used to provide the melody for curriculum songs.

"Michael, Row the Boat Ashore"

"She'll Be Comin' Round the Mountain"

"This Old Man"

"Pop Goes the Weasel"

"Clementine"

"Oh, Susannah"

"The Wheels on the Bus"

"London Bridge"

"We Shall Overcome"

"Jimmy Crack Corn"

"This Land is Your Land"

"When the Saints Go Marching In"

"When Johnny Comes Marching Home"

"Sarasponda"

"The Battle Hymn of the Republic"

"The Old Gray Mare"

"Alouette"

"My Country, 'Tis of Thee"

"Camptown Races"

"I've Been Working on the Railroad"

"Hava Nagila"

"Puff, the Magic Dragon"

"Twinkle, Twinkle Little Star"

"Yankee Doodle"

Interpersonal Strategies to Differentiate

1. Working in cooperative groups, students teach each other parts of a lesson. Each student is responsible for teaching only one part, while everyone learns the whole lesson collaboratively.

2. To develop the ability to resolve disputes and negotiate conflicts, students practice conflict resolution techniques with either simulated or actual problems.

3. Students practice critiquing one another's work to learn how to give and receive feedback.

4. To build collaborative skills and to share each other's areas of expertise, students work on group projects together, each assuming a role according to his or her strengths.

5. Students engage in school or community service activities to develop values such as empathy, respect, altruism, and sharing.

6. To understand others and appreciate differences, students study diverse cultures, including customs, beliefs, and values.

7. Use the "Think-Pair-Share" technique to engage students in reflecting upon a class topic and the or the "Turn and Talk" (to a partner) technique for discussing their thoughts with a partner.

8. To understand differing points of view, students assume various positions and debate a complex issue.

9. Students interview persons with special talents to learn about their areas of specialty as well as how to interview others effectively.

10. To learn from the expertise of others, students work as a apprentices with community experts.

Sample Interpersonal Activity: Mix-and-Match Grouping

This grouping activity works well for introducing new material. The teacher organizes students into groups of four or five and hands out a set of numbered (1–5) fact cards to each group. Each card in a set should have different information about the subject, and each group's set of cards should be the same.

Students read their cards then move to new groups with matching numbers. (All the 1's get together; all the 2's get together, etc.) These groups then plan a strategy to teach their original groups what they have learned from their cards.

When the groups are ready, students return to their original group. Now everyone has a different piece of the puzzle and a method for teaching it. Individuals take turns sharing their piece with their group.

Intrapersonal Strategies to Differentiate

1. At the beginning of a course, school year or semester, students establish personal short- and long-term learning goals.

2. Students maintain portfolios to evaluate their own learning.

3. Using schedules, timelines, and planning strategies, students choose and direct some of their own learning activities to gain autonomous learning skills.

4. Students keep daily learning logs in which they express their emotional reactions to lessons and share insights they have about the content.

5. Students explain why certain units of study are valuable for them both in and out of school.

6. Students select a particular value, such as kindness or determination, and incorporate that value into their behavior for a week at a time.

7. To enhance self-esteem, students practice giving and receiving compliments.

8. At least once per quarter, students pursue an independent project of their choice, spanning between two and three weeks.

9. Students write autobiographies to explain how class content has enhanced their understanding of themselves.

10. Students use teacher's feedback and self-assessment inventories to reflect on their individual learning, thinking, and problem-solving strategies.

Sample Intrapersonal Activity: Student Options

One approach to empowering students academically, while developing intrapersonal skills, is to encourage them to make choices involving their educational experiences. Choices can be open ended, based on student interests, or they can be provided by the teacher. A few suggestions are listed below for enabling students to construct their learning experiences:

Students decide how best to organize the classroom's physical layout.

Students choose topics for reading and writing assignments.

Students select from a range of options for independent research projects.

Students offer input for the daily schedule.

Students develop rules and discipline policies for common problems that arise.

Students choose seating arrangement.

Teacher shows students how to set goals for themselves and provides opportunities for them to complete the goals they have set.

Teacher provides frequent opportunities for self-reflection and self-evaluation.

Teacher supplies students with personal journals and plans a regular journal-writing time.

Students determine the criteria by which their work will be assessed.

Naturalist Strategies to Differentiate

1. Students make collections of rocks, shells, bugs, leaves, feathers or other natural objects; or of cards, beads, or small figures. They are encouraged to categorize these items by their characteristics in common.

2. Students are asked to closely observe changes in nature. They can observe a single tree outside the classroom window, the weather, a park, or life cycles of plants or animals.

3. Teachers ask students to recognize patterns in natural objects: lines, shapes, repetitions, or cycles.

4. Students are encouraged to use binoculars, telescopes, or microscopes to observe natural phenomena.

5. Students sort, organize, and categorize rocks, shells, or other natural objects and label the categories.

6. Students reflect on the local or global environment and plan environmentally conscious activities.

7. Students visit a local animal shelter or find ways to help abandoned pets.

8. Using local flora or fauna, students create a taxonomy, or system by which to categorize them.

9. Students grow plants from seeds and observe and record their changes over time.

10. Students forecast and track the weather.

11. Students observe the sky, clouds, stars, and space.

12. Students give reports on nature videos or photograph nature.

13. Students go on field trips to natural settings, take nature walks, or hike in natural settings.

Sample Naturalist Activity: Creating a Class Garden

Although most schools do not have garden space available for class projects, there are many creative ways to design and even create one, including miniature gardens, container gardens, and hydroponic gardens.

Growing plants in recycled soda bottles is an easy way to create a miniature hydroponics growing system in the classroom. The plants are watered from a reservoir situated below them. Several plants can grow in a two-liter-bottle garden. The gardens can be supervised by individual students or small groups. The following materials are needed:

■ One 2-liter soda bottle (one-liter bottle can also be used for a smaller growing system)

■ One bottle cap, or aluminum foil and rubber band to cover bottle opening

■ A tool for making a hole in the bottle cap, or aluminum foil

■ Wicking material-fabric interfacing or cotton string

■ Planting medium (a soil-less mixture of approximately one part peat moss and one part vermiculite)

■ Fertilizer: solid pellets added during planting or liquid fertilizer mixed and kept in the water reservoir throughout the life cycle

■ Packet of seeds

■ Water

When beginning Multiple Intelligences–based teaching, many teachers select intelligence strategies listed above and put them together in a worksheet, so that students have multiple ways to learn academic content. Two sample worksheets are provided on the following pages: one on spelling and one on multiplication.

Differentiating Spelling Using MI

The following list provides you with a variety of ways to practice spelling words at school and at home. Select the strategies that you enjoy most and vary these strategies each week. Try to determine which approaches best help you learn the spelling words.

Logical–mathematical strategy: List your spelling words from shortest to longest or longest to shortest; from fewest syllables to most syllables or vice versa; in alphabetical or in reverse alphabetical order; by the number of vowels or consonants; or with acronyms formed from the first letters of words.

Visual strategy: Write your words using different colors for different letters, for vowels and consonants, or for different words. Draw or paste pictures next to each word as a visual reminder.

Linguistic strategy: Make up a story using all your spelling words. Tell the story to another person, stopping to spell out each spelling word.

Musical strategy: Sing-spell your words to the melody of your favorite song.

Kinesthetic strategy: Create a "body alphabet" of letters and pantomime the letters of each spelling word.

Interpersonal strategy: With a partner, use the Think-Pair-Share technique or Turn and Talk technique to practice your spelling words.

Naturalist activity: Create associations between animals, birds, fish, insects, flowers, or trees and your spelling words. For example, the word *yellow* could be associated with "yak": *a yellow yak*; the word *button* could be associated with "butterfly": *a butterfly button*; the word *cannot* could be associated with "carrot": *I cannot eat a carrot*.

Differentiating Multiplication Using MI

The following list provides you with a variety of ways to practice multiplication at school and at home. Select the strategies that you enjoy the most and vary the strategies each week. Try to determine which approaches helped you learn multiplication the best.

Visual strategy: With a partner, play the paper-plate game to practice your multiplication facts. Write answers to the multiplication tables, one per plate, and place the plates on the floor. Have your partner call out a problem—for example, 6 × 3. You would jump onto the plate with the correct answer: 18.

Make artistic flash cards for each multiplication fact. For example, you could draw twenty-four flowers on one side of the card and on the flip side have the statement 6 × 4.

Linguistic strategy: Make up mini-stories with multiplication facts in them. For example, one story might begin, "There once was a boy who played basketball and scored four points per basket."

Logical–mathematical strategy: When looking at a chart of the multiplication facts, find at least two number patterns in the chart.

Musical strategy: Create a simple, repetitive jingle about multiplication facts; e.g., 6 × 6 is 36, 7 × 7 is 49, etc.

Interpersonal strategy: Interview other people to find out how they memorized the multiplication tables. Take tips from them that will help you to memorize these math facts.

Intrapersonal intelligence: Keep a daily log to express your feelings about learning the multiplication tables and to track which facts you learn each day.

Naturalist strategy: Use pebbles, seeds, or other natural objects to make number families; for example, four rows of pebbles by six rows. How many pebbles are in four columns by six rows?

Part IV

Differentiating Assessment in an MI Classroom

In my own classroom, I have found it necessary to design alternative assessment processes that reflect the MI work of my students. I have learned that it is valuable to engage in "collaborative assessment conferences" with my students, so that they can discuss the criteria by which their work is assessed. I have developed portfolio processes, evaluation forms, self-reflection sheets, and MI-report cards to record students' progress. Such methods of assessment are included in this section.

I would also like to point out that, just as we can teach in multiple ways, we can also assess in multiple ways. MI assessments can take a variety of forms. Students can demonstrate their learning through original songs, essays, group presentations, and project presentations, or through visuals, such as charts, diagrams, or timelines. In addition, a teacher's assessment repertoire should include peer- and self-assessment processes. The assessment sections of each lesson plan in this book contain examples of assessment ideas.

Whenever I assess my students, I also remind myself that assessment serves many purposes. First, it documents a student's progress and provides a way to communicate with students and others about that progress. Second, assessment is an important feedback tool—not just concerning student progress but also my effectiveness as a teacher. It encourages me to reflect on what works in my teaching and what needs to improve. Third, assessment gives me insight into the strengths and challenges of each student and asks me to identify appropriate interventions. In my mind, assessment is an ongoing dialogue, not a final, summative event.

Part IV Contents

- An MI Rubric
- The Collaborative Assessment Conference
- MI Portfolios to Differentiate Assessment
- Personal Reflection Sheets
- Peer-Assessment: The Appreciation Sandwich
- Assessment of Student Projects
- A Multiple Intelligences Report Card

An MI Rubric

Teachers often create both teaching and assessment materials for each curriculum unit they cover. I have found it convenient at times to have a generic rubric ready for quick adaptation to any lesson I teach. I've developed the following rubric for just such a purpose. It can be completed by teacher, students, or both. It can also serve as a cover sheet for a portfolio item.

Student Name: _____

Assignment: _____

Date: _____

	OUTSTANDING	GOOD	FAIR	NEEDS WORK
Content				
Demonstrated understanding of important concepts				
Provided examples of important concepts				
Addressed state standards				
Skills				
Showed evidence of research skills				
Effectively communicated content to audience				
Used at least three intelligences in presentation				
Articulated challenges in completing assignment				

The Collaborative Assessment Conference

The collaborative assessment conference, originally designed for Arts PROPEL at Harvard's Project Zero, is a dialogue between student and teacher about important student work. It democratizes the assessment process by giving those who are being assessed an opportunity to say what the assessment should look like and, upon completion of their work, how they think that they met that criteria. The assumption of this conference is that serious work deserves serious attention and response. Collaborative assessment conferences have two aspects: the first is to determine criteria for assessing student work, and the second is to reflect, in depth, on the effectiveness of that work.

Establishing Assessment Criteria

Before students tackle an important assignment or major project, the teacher and students should hold an assessment conference. This will require between ten and thirty minutes of discussion. The purpose of the conference is to establish the criteria for assessing students' work. While the class discusses what an assessment should consist of, the teacher should list the criteria upon the board. It is important that these criteria address both content and skill development. For example, one requirement might be that the completed assignment reveals a clear understanding of an important concept; a second requirement might be that the concept is effectively presented in a graph, chart, or diagram; a third requirement might be that the concept is applied to a real-world situation.

By establishing their own criteria in advance, students have familiar guidelines for their work. They no longer need to guess what the teacher expects from them, and they know exactly what their responsibilities entail. It is also helpful if teachers have examples of prior students' work to share as models. By seeing what others have done, students are in a better position to make decisions about what they might do. Rather than encouraging copying, examples encourage students to build on the ideas of others and to forge their own problem-solving approaches. Presenting previous projects often increases the quality of students' efforts and products significantly.

Assessing Student Work

Upon completion of an important assignment, the second collaborative assessment conference is scheduled. The purpose of this conference is to provide feedback about the quality of the student's work, about how well the student met the criteria, and about how the teacher can help the student succeed further. Occasionally, other participants, such as teachers, specialists, parents, or other students, may also be included in this conference. The teacher can conduct these conferences with individual students or with the entire class observing and participating in the individual assessment. Before the assessment conference begins, it is critical that the teacher reads or examines the student's final work in order to be prepared to discuss it. During the conference, it is important that the student who completes the work also discusses the project.

I have suggested some topics below that may be helpful to the teacher in conducting an assessment conference:

1. In the simplest terms and without judgment, the teacher describes what the student has created.

2. The teacher shares an opinion about the most striking aspect of this project. The focus here should be on description and not on why the student completed the work in a particular manner.

3. The teacher poses questions about the work and the student's work process.

4. The teacher evaluates how well the work addresses the criteria.

During the conference, the student and any conference participants should be encouraged to discuss the work. The teacher can facilitate discussion with questions that encourage students to respond to the teacher's feedback: "Have any of my comments about the project surprised you, given the criteria?"; "Do you have any observations you would like to add?"; "Are there aspects of your work that I have not taken into account when assessing the project?"

To conclude a collaborative assessment conference, the teacher should suggest subsequent steps in the student's learning. Even though the student has a finished product, one of the important concepts to communicate is that learning is an ongoing and unending process. Some suggested comments and questions follow:

1. I believe this work demonstrates that you have a strength in _____ that you can apply to other work.

2. Do you have additional interests that you would like to pursue because of this project?

3. Now that you have completed this assignment, what aspects of it do you think could be strengthened?

4. What encourages you to do high-quality work in the future?

5. What goals can you set for your future work?

In closing the conference, the teacher will find it worthwhile to discuss the conference itself: How did it benefit everyone involved? How could it be improved? Finally, it is important to end on a positive note. Comments like "I can see that you learned a lot from creating your chart" are helpful in encouraging ongoing effort.

MI Portfolios to Differentiate Assessment

Portfolios of students' work are becoming increasingly popular with both elementary and secondary teachers. I have experimented with portfolio systems that consisted of a collection folder, which included each student's work, and a showcase portfolio, which contained only selected pieces. When selecting pieces for placement in a portfolio, the teacher must maintain a balanced ratio of teacher-chosen work to student-chosen work.

I have also experimented with different categories of portfolios, depending on the subject area. At times I have asked my students to maintain a single subject or topic portfolio, such as a science portfolio or a writing portfolio. At other times I have worked with comprehensive portfolios that incorporate work from all content areas. In any case, the portfolio can cover the work of one term, an entire year, or it can follow the student from year to year.

Depending upon the anticipated size of my students' portfolios, they are stored in either a folder or box. My students' portfolios typically contain not only their work but assessment records for selected items, such as Personal Reflection Sheets and rubrics that evaluate the chosen pieces.

I like to use portfolios because they are not only folders of students' work and processes but are also valuable assessment tools. They can chart students' progress in a limited way—over the course of one assignment—or they can reveal comprehensive growth by showing students' work over the course of the school year or term. For example, with some writing assignments, I ask my students to include their rough drafts, edited copies, and final copies, thus revealing the steps used to complete an assignment.

While I use portfolios for assessment purposes, students look at their portfolios for feedback on ways to improve their work. In this way, students acquire a sense of ownership of the ongoing learning process. Other forms of assessment often fail to incorporate this form of reflection.

In my classroom, I try to ensure that portfolios incorporate evidence of work from several intelligences. Over the years I have assigned the following portfolio entries. This list might present possibilities for your students' portfolios as well:

- All forms of written work including drafts, peer-edited versions, teacher-edited versions and final copies of creative writing, research papers, poetry, and reports

- Math assignments, including calculations and problem-solving

- Paintings, drawings, designs

- Charts, graphs, diagrams

- Photographs of sculptures, constructions, sewing, etc.

- Musical scores

- Audiotapes of musical performances

- Videotapes of plays, dances, interviews, presentations

- Learning logs

- Personal reflection sheets

- Rubrics and other evaluation forms

- Project contracts

- Statements of personal goals

- Checklists for classroom tasks

- Research notes

- Computer-generated work (spreadsheets, databases, graphics, etc.)

- Peer- or parent-feedback forms

Personal Reflection Sheets

One of the most important aspects of differentiated assessment in an MI classroom is teaching students how to assess their own work. Even very young students can develop reflective skills when trained to do so.

Reflection helps students develop editorial skills, identify the strengths and weaknesses of their work, and manage their individual learning. I have used the following two forms—the Personal Reflection Sheet and the Self-Assessment Sheet—with my students when I want them to reflect on work that is to be included in their portfolios, or when I want them to evaluate the quality of work produced for a specific assignment.

Personal Reflection Sheet

(Use for work to be included in your portfolio.)

Name: _____   Date: _____

Title of piece: _____

1. Description of piece: _____
   _____
   _____

2. What did you learn from working on this assignment? _____
   _____
   _____

3. What did you learn about yourself from working on this piece?
   _____
   _____
   _____

4. What could be done to enhance your work? _____
   _____
   _____

5. What challenges or problems did you encounter? _____
   _____
   _____

6. Does this work meet the specified criteria? Why or why not?
   _____
   _____
   _____

7. In what ways does this work encourage you to study more about
   this topic? _____
   _____
   _____

Student Self-Assessment Sheet

(Use to assess your work on designated assignments.)

Name: _____   Date: _____

Assignment: _____

1. What was your goal for this assignment?

    _____

    _____

2. How well did you accomplish your goal?

    _____

    _____

3. What is the best part of your work on this assignment?

    _____

    _____

4. What part(s) of your work might need improvement?

    _____

    _____

5. What was your least favorite activity when working on this
    assignment? _____

    _____

6. What did you learn about yourself while working on this?_____

    _____

    _____

7. If you did the assignment over, how would it be different?

    _____

    _____

8. How does this assignment connect with work in this or other
    classes? _____

    _____

9. Based on the criteria, what score or grade do you think this work
    deserves? Why? _____

    _____

Peer-Assessment:
The Appreciation Sandwich

After class presentations, I always invite my students to critique each other. Students can be taught to provide constructive feedback with tact and diplomacy. In my classroom, feedback is built into daily activities. At the completion of time in the learning centers, students volunteer to share the products they have created that day. Individuals and groups informally share their reading, writing, art work, skits, models, and songs. After the sharing is completed, the rest of the class comments on strong and weak points in the various presentations.

A second and more formal opportunity for feedback occurs when students present their independent projects. Each student receives constructive criticism. The presenter's classmates and I offer criticism based on the criteria established for that assignment. One technique my students use to critique each other is the appreciation sandwich. In an appreciation sandwich a critical comment is sandwiched between two positive comments. For example, if one of my students, Kristi, were presenting on Medieval castles, I might give her the following appreciation sandwich about her presentation:

> Kristi, I enjoyed your presentation on Medieval castles. It was an interesting topic for me because I never knew how they lived in those castles. Your eye contact needs work. You kept looking down at the floor, and I wanted you to look up at me. Your visuals were great; in particular, the chart that showed the insides of castles. That helped me understand how the people got around and how they lived.

Human nature being what it is, Kristi will remember the criticism, but she will also—hopefully—remember the positive input as well.

During my years of teaching, I have observed that appreciation sandwiches are as effective as any assessment in encouraging change in students' work. Consistently, students follow through with each other's recommendations, as well as continue to build upon their identified strengths.

Assessment of Student Projects

Since my students are required to do several major projects during each school year, I wanted to determine whether the quality of each student's projects had improved over time. I became curious about whether students had consistently relied on one or two intelligences to communicate their learning, whether their research skills had improved, and whether their projects had grown more sophisticated.

To secure such information, I developed the following rubric. On cardstock, I photocopy one rubric per student and use it as one assessment device for monthly project presentations. The cardstock is sturdy enough to last the entire school year. I maintain these records for the students to use, so that they, too, can track their progress from project to project, over the course of the school year. The students themselves have input into categories on the rubric.

Project Evaluation Sheet

Name: _____

CRITERIA	PROJECT								COMMENTS
	1	2	3	4	5	6	7	8	
Began with effective introduction									
Was well organized									
Did effective research									
Understood major concepts									
Provided good supporting data									
Offered good examples and elaboration of content									
Had a strong closing									
Used effective presentation skills									
Included visual aids									
Included music									
Included a kinesthetic component									
Included interpersonal elements									
Included intrapersonal elements									
Included logical–mathematical components									
Included effective linguistic components									

A Multiple Intelligences Report Card

Not only have some of my daily assessment processes changed, so has my report card. Once I started my MI classroom model, I soon realized that the traditional report card failed to assess the work my students were actually doing. To better reflect our classroom efforts, I created the following report card. This report attempts to portray the developmental level of each student in all eight intelligences, through a bar-graph format. I use a different color for each of the four marking periods, and I attempt to show whether a student is developmentally a novice, an apprentice, a practitioner, or a scholar for each criterion. Naturally, the categories can be changed.

In the event that a student does not progress in an area between marking periods, I draw a vertical line to represent static development in that criterion. Most students, however, continue to grow in each of the areas over the course of a school year. Sometimes I make brief narrative comments below each bar if appropriate. A section is designated at the end for follow-up suggestions. Here I recommend what parents may do to enhance the strengths of their child and to remediate any apparent weaknesses.

A
MULTIPLE
INTELLIGENCES
REPORT CARD
FOR

Student _____

Multiple Intelligences Report Card with Developmental Indicators

Name: _____

	BEGINNER	AMATEUR	PRACTITIONER	AUTHORITY	FOLLOW-UP SUGGESTIONS
Reading (Verbal–Linguistic Intelligence)					
Writing (Verbal–Linguistic Intelligence)					
Math and Science (Logical–Mathematical Intelligence)					
Movement and Exercise Bodily–Kinesthetic Intelligence)					
Building Activities (Bodily–Kinesthetic Intelligence)					
Musical Activities (Musical–Rhythmic Intelligences)					
Visual Arts Activities (Visual–Spatial Intelligence)					
Group Work (Interpersonal Intelligence)					
Reflective Thinking (Intrapersonal Intelligence)					
Nature-Related Activities (Naturalist Intelligence)					
Project Work (Project Preparation and Demonstration)					

Beginner: recognizes basic concepts, begins to develop skills
Amateur: increases skills through instruction and guided practice
Practitioner: works independently and accurately with knowledge and skill
Authority: demonstrates mastery of concepts and practices; applies in new settings

(Colored bars demonstrate beginning points in each area and extent of progress up to time report card is released. The longer the line, the greater the improvement. New colors represent new grading periods.)

Part V

Differentiated Lessons Using MI

Whenever I do workshops for teachers on differentiated instruction and Multiple Intelligences, I am frequently asked, "Do you have prepared lesson plans that you could share with me?" This section of the handbook is filled with lessons for a variety of subject areas. The contents of this section begin with Lesson 2, because the first lesson is included in Part II.

Part V Contents

Lesson Format

These lessons can be taught to students in a number of ways. The students may work in groups at learning centers or as a whole class. The timeframe can also vary: some lessons may be completed in one hour, one day, or last one week or one month. The lessons presented here may also serve as parts of larger units and broader themes. For example, a lesson on Christopher Columbus could be integrated into a unit on the Age of Exploration.

In addition, lesson sections can be divided into dozens of individual MI activities for the classroom. The teacher should determine what to teach and when. The sequence of activities within the lessons, as presented here, does not dictate the order in which they might be taught. For example, even though the lessons all begin with linguistic activities, the teacher may want to begin with the kinesthetic or visual activities. In short, teachers should feel free to use any sequence that they find suitable.

Finally, it is not essential to teach every lesson in eight ways. Teachers are encouraged to pick and choose activities that fit their particular lessons on any given day. However, it is important to provide opportunities for students to engage each of the intelligences for at least some time during each broad unit of study.

Lesson 2: Adjectives

Subject Area: Language Arts

State Standard: Correct Use of Modifiers

Principle Taught: Written or oral language is enhanced with descriptive words.

Unit: Parts of Speech

Grade Level: 3–8

Materials Needed: graph paper, large blank cards, paper and colored markers, five to eight large sheets of butcher paper, written text with several adjectives for assessment activity

Linguistic Activity

On the blackboard, the teacher lists several adjectives. Incorporating these adjectives, students write phrases or sentences on a topic suggested by the teacher or by students.

Younger students might be given a written story with blanks. In this variation, the students' task would be to fill in the blanks with adjectives from a list on the chalkboard or with their own adjectives.

Logical–Mathematical Activity

Students count the number of adjectives, nouns, and verbs in a given piece of text. The teacher might ask one of the class's best writers whether there are predictable ratios for parts of speech; e.g, more nouns than verbs, more adjectives than adverbs. (This activity assumes that students have previously studied at least some parts of speech.) A sample chart is provided for quantifying the parts of speech.

	NUMBER OF NOUNS	NUMBER OF VERBS	NUMBER OF ADJECTIVES
paragraph 1			
paragraph 2			
paragraph 3			
paragraph 4			
paragraph 5			
paragraph 6			

Next, students might compare the numbers of each part of speech by drawing a bar graph or pie chart. This can be done on graph paper or on the computer. A sample graph is demonstrated in the figure below.

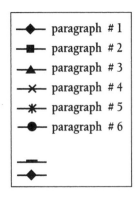
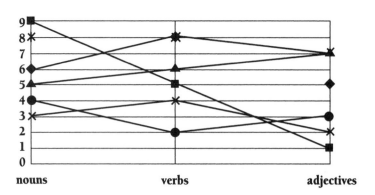

Kinesthetic Activity

To prepare this activity, the teacher will need to write several sentences with one word per large, blank card. When class begins, the teacher distributes several blank cards to each student and asks for volunteers to stand in front of the class with the word cards that the teacher has prepared. Each volunteer should have one card, and the volunteer group should form a sentence to display for the class. The seated students write adjectives on their word cards that would make fitting substitutions for the adjective(s) in the displayed sentence. Students raise their hands and, when called on, move to the front of the class inserting their adjectives into the sentence. Other students may also move to the front of the classroom, tap an "adjective" on the shoulder, and replace it in the displayed sentence. The same process could be adapted to individual student work: students use smaller word cards at their desks with teacher- or textbook-provided sentences. In some clases, students working in groups can make their own cards for other groups to use in constructing sentences.

Visual–Spatial Activity

Students create a circle map for describing nouns with adjectives. A circle map is simply a web or mindmap with one circle in the middle, adjoined by smaller circles containing adjectives.

It is important for students to realize that only adjectives—words that describe—can go in the circles on a circle map. For visual thinkers, this turns out to be a useful tool for creating mental images that correspond to written words.

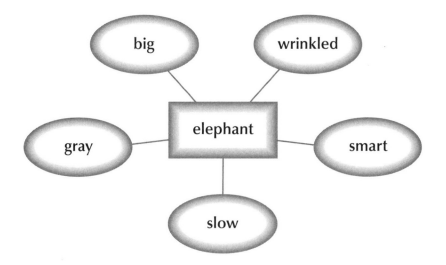

Musical Activity

Students choose a song that they all know and change the adjectives in its lyrics. For example, "Mary had a little lamb. / Its fleece was white as snow." would work well with young children. Teachers can call on different students to voice replacements for "little" or "white" while students sing. This can be done in combination with the word cards in the kinesthetic activity above.

Interpersonal Activity

Working in groups of four or five, students choose a mascot, select four or five adjectives to describe that mascot, and then illustrate the mascot on butcher paper. Each student in the group is responsible for depicting one of the mascot's characteristics based upon the adjectives offered by each group member.

For example, one group might choose an alien as its mascot and, over the course of the exercise, become the green, slimy, toothy, ugly, smiley aliens. The group members would then draw their green, slimy, toothy, ugly, smiley alien, each student coloring in the trait that corresponds to the adjective individually offered.

Next, each group holds up its picture for the class to see. The other students attempt to guess the five adjectives used to describe the group's mascot.

Intrapersonal Activity

To increase intrapersonal awareness, students make individual lists of adjectives to describe themselves, or write stories about themselves.

To extend the lesson one step further, the teacher might ask students each to explain why they chose the adjectives they did. For example, "I am a sad person. The reason I am sad is my dog died last week, and I miss her. I am also a responsible person. The reason I am responsible is I like to do my chores without anyone asking me to."

Naturalist Activity

There are an endless number of natural objects (trees, animals, insects, rocks, plants, bugs, etc.) that are worthy of description. As an exercise in using adjectives, the teacher puts students in pairs and assigns each roles A and B. The teacher asks the A person to select an animal, plant, or natural object and the B person to select an adjective, then asks the pair to put the words together.

(For example, a gigantic cat.) Students in each pair then switch roles, and B selects an animal, plant, or natural object, and A selects the modifier.

Assessment

With a colored marker, students underline all adjectives in a written selection. They then trade papers with a partner and correct each other's paper with a marker of a different color.

Lesson 3: Magnetism

Subject Area: Science

State Standard: Forces in Nature

Principle Taught: Magnetic fields are comprised of attraction and repulsion forces.

Unit: Physical Science (Electricity and Magnetism)

Grade Level: 3–10

Materials Needed: printed material with information on magnets and magnetism, magnets of various sizes and shapes, paper clips, pins, nails, iron filings, one or more small postal scales, percussion instruments

Optional Materials: small boxes, wire, compasses

Linguistic Activity

In a scientific text, encyclopedia, or library book, students read about magnets and magnetism. Many sources describe or illustrate the magnetic fields of a variety of magnets. After reading the selection, students might answer describe how magnets are made, how they work, what causes magnetism, and how magnets of different shapes are used.

Logical–Mathematical Activity

Working with magnets of different sizes and shapes, students try to pick up as many paper clips or other metal objects as they can. They count how many clips each magnet attracts and record their findings. For variety, the teacher might suggest that students weigh the clips on small postal scales and then compare the weight of the objects each gathered. Students might also attempt to attract pins, nails, or other objects to determine whether magnetic strength varies from object to object.

Kinesthetic Activity

Students experiment with magnets and various magnetic and non-magnetic objects by playing with them, observing their properties and strengths. The teacher then asks students to observe in a more deliberate manner which objects are magnetic.

One excellent activity suggested in many science books asks students to make their own electromagnets, to see the magnetic effects of electricity. To demonstrate how to make an electro-magnet, the teacher wraps wire several times around a small jewelry-size box, forming a coil. The teacher next strips the insulation from the ends of the wire and connect the wires to the terminals of a dry cell battery. The teacher then places a compass inside the box and turns the box so that the compass's needle lines up with the wire. The students observe how the compass needle moves.

If the ends of the wire are switched back and forth between the terminals at just the right speed, the needle on the compass spins. Students then attempt to explain the phenomenon they observe.

Visual–Spatial Activity

Working in small groups, students map the field of a bar magnet by placing an iron magnet under a sheet of white paper and sprinkling iron filings on the paper. When the paper is gently tapped, the filings flow into a very distinct pattern, radiating away from the magnetic poles. Students draw similar patterns with charcoal or pencil and explain why this happens.

For variation, students place two bar magnets under the paper and observe different patterns made by the filings, depending on whether the poles of the two magnets are attracting or repelling each other. Students can also draw these patterns and identify the poles of the magnets: N and N or S and S if the poles are alike, N and S if they are different.

Musical Activity

The teacher provides students, in small groups, with drums, tambourines, rhythm sticks, or other percussion instruments and asks them to create an attracting and repelling melody. Attracting melodies might have two instruments (or two groups of instruments) alternating their sounds. Repelling melodies might play simultaneously. Or attracting rhythms might include an echo (one student beats a rhythm and others imitate it), while repelling rhythms are dissimilar.

Interpersonal Activity

Students stand in pairs, with arms crossed on their chests to pantomime magnets and their fields. The teacher calls out directions every few seconds:

> You are both magnets. Your arms are your positive pole, your back is your negative pole. The magnetism is turned off until I say "on." Stand about three feet apart, facing each other: On. Off. Now one person turns halfway around so that all partners are situated front to back: On. Off. Now the other person turns, so that all partners are back to back: On. Off.

Directions can continue until students understand the concept. Variation can be added with *high-low, fast-flow, smooth-jerky, big-small,* and other elements of movement. The addition of music can turn the activity from into a dance of magnets.

Intrapersonal Activity

Ask students to reflect individually in their journals on magnetic phenomena in their lives. Provide starter sentences as follows:

> I am attracted to …
>
> I am repelled by …

Naturalist Activity

To help students understand magnetism as a natural force, the teachers asks students simply to observe and experience the force between two magnets. The overlap with the kinesthetic activity is obvious, but the purpose of this activity is that students feel the force of magnetism. Students can also experiment with magnets and a variety of different magnetic and nonmagnetic objects, and predict which will be attracted to the magnets and which will not.

Assessment

To help students demonstrate their understanding of magnetism as natural force, the teacher provides students with magnets, metal filings, and other magnetic and nonmagnetic objects, then has them create their own experiment to demonstrate the principles of magnetism. They can work individually or in small groups to demonstrate what is happening and to explain why magnetism occurs.

Lesson 4: Adding Fractions

Subject Area: Math

State Standard: Mathematics Involves Numbers and Parts of Numbers

Principle Taught: Parts of a whole can be combined.

Unit: Fractions

Grade Level: 4–6

Materials Needed: copies of the fraction stories (in the linguistic activity), sheets of music, beans or other manipulatives, one piece of cardstock per student

Linguistic Activity

Provide copies of the following two fractions-focused stories to students. Ask them to illustrate the images described in the stories.

Maria suddenly found herself in the land of fractions. There was one-half of a house, two-thirds of a mountain, and one-fourth of a tree. Even the animals were fractional. She saw a dog with only three-fourths of its legs and an elephant with four-fifths of a trunk. The weirdest thing was a bird with only half its wings—one wing, that is—that kept flying around in circles.

The old train crept up the mountain. It was 204 miles to the top. After three hours it passed the halfway marker so the engineer knew that he was halfway to the top. But now the mountain was steeper and the train slowed even more. After another three hours it was halfway from that last marker to the top. How far is the train from the top of the mountain?

Once students have read and illustrated the two stories, they create their own fraction word problems or stories.

Logical–Mathematical Activity

Ask students to pretend that they are math-textbook authors. They must create, in their own words, formulas for adding fractions and provide examples of their formulas.

Kinesthetic Activity

Many manipulatives, such as blocks, counters, and beans, can be used for fractions. In the absence of manipulatives, the teacher or students can make simple sets of fractions from paper cut into pizza-like shapes.

    In one sample activity the teacher gives each student twenty-four beans and asks them to divide the group of beans in half, then one of those halves in half again. Students should now have three piles, one of twelve beans and two of six. The teacher explains that each of the two smaller piles represents one-fourth of the total pile. The teacher then asks the students that, if they add one-forth to the other one-fourth, they will have how many beans; and what fraction this is of the total.

Visual–Spatial Activity

Students can make fraction strips out of cardstock. Each student should cut out five strips, about two inches by twelve inches, as shown.

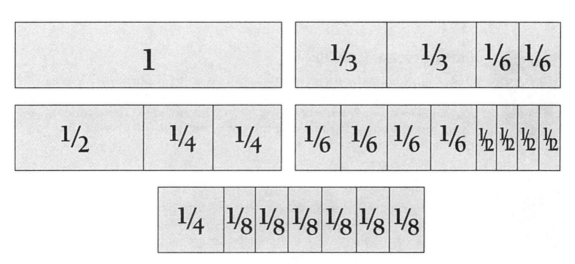

    After labeling the parts of each strip, the teacher directs the students to cut them into their fractional parts. Pieces should be labeled with students' names on the back and kept in an envelope so they don't get lost. (Fraction strip games are described in the interpersonal activity below.)

Musical Activity

Studying fractions offers a perfect time to learn to read music. The teacher provides students with sheets of music and shows them quarter notes, half notes, and whole notes. Once they have learned these three symbols, they can progress to making music by clapping or using rhythm sticks. The teacher or a student can clap out a steady rhythm (whole notes), with the class echoing the leader. Then the class claps in double time (half notes) and quadruple time (quarter notes).

Interpersonal Activity

Games using the fraction strips from the preceding visual–spatial activity are described here. The games are for two to four players.

Make a Whole

1. Players mix their fractional parts into one pile.
2. Each player takes out one fractional part per turn, until all parts are gone.
3. Each player tries to make as many whole "ones" as possible by placing pieces on the uncut strip.

Pairs

1. Players work in pairs, mixing their cards into one pile.
2. The teacher sets a time limit (two–four minutes).
3. Teams put together as many halves as possible within the time limit.

Take Ten

1. Players work in groups of three or four.
2. Each player selects ten fraction parts and puts them into a group pile.
3. As a group, the players try to make as many whole ones as possible.

Intrapersonal Activity

Ask students to write their favorite activities on the back of each piece of fraction strip (e.g., playing video games, reading, listening to music, playing football, talking on the telephone, eating ice cream, etc.). Then students fit their pieces together to make one full day of activities. One whole day can hold only so many parts.

Naturalist Activity

The kinesthetic activities above can be done with natural objects: small pebbles, shells, cones, sticks, pine needles, or leaves. Students can gather their own sets of pebbles, etc., and keep them in small boxes nearby for various fraction activities.

Assessment

Working individually or in pairs, students mix all their fraction strips into one pile. They demonstrate their understanding of fractions by reassembling all five (or ten, if they are working in pairs) of their strips into wholes. To increase the challenge, make this a timed activity. To add variety, the pieces can all be placed face-down so that students have to reassemble the parts visually. It is important for teacher and students to realize that there is more than one correct method of completing this task.

Lesson 5: Christopher Columbus

Subject Area: Social Studies

State Standard: Exploration

Principle Taught: Explorations affect native cultures.

Unit: Early American History

Grade Level: 3–8

Materials Needed: contrasting written accounts of Christopher Columbus's New World voyage, butcher paper, world map and digital projector, Caribbean and European music (see musical activity)

Linguistic Activity

Many social studies textbooks describe the voyages of Columbus from one point of view. A great resource that offers an alternative perspective on Columbus's arrival in the Americas is *A People's History of the United States* by Howard Zinn. Students learn from Zinn's account in the first chapter that Columbus was both a great explorer and a ruthless conqueror who invaded the land of the Arawaks and nearly destroyed their culture. Students might read contrasting accounts of Columbus's life and then attempt to reconcile them: why he is generally portrayed as a hero, the contributions he made, and his impact on Native Americans.

Logical–Mathematical Activity

Studying Columbus's Atlantic voyage provides students with opportunities to study maps and scales, as well as math problems addressing distance, rate, and time. Teachers may want to provide students with the following data:

- Columbus traveled over 4,000 miles.

- It took him thirty-six days to cross the Atlantic on the outward journey and fifty-eight days on the return.

- His lead ship, the *Santa Maria*, was about eighty feet long and carried only forty men.

- Modern ocean-going ships are often over one thousand feet long and can carry over three thousand passengers.

Such facts provide ample material for mathematical problem-solving. Some sample problems for students to solve might include:

1. If Columbus left the Canary Islands on August 12, 1492, and landed in the Bahamas on October 12, how many days was he at sea?

2. If the *Pinta*, the *Niña*, and the *Santa Maria* traveled 4,286 miles in thirty-six days, what was the average number of miles traveled per day?

3. Columbus started out with ninety men. Seven of them died on the trip west. Fifteen of them stayed in the Bahamas. Nine Arawaks were loaded onto the ships before the return to Europe. Nineteen were lost in a storm on the return voyage, and twelve of the crew deserted in the Azores. How many men returned to Portugal with him?

4. The *Santa Maria* was eighty feet long, the *Pinta* was seventy-two feet long, and the *Niña* was sixty-seven feet long. If they were anchored, bow to stern, in a harbor, at least how long would the harbor have to be to fit all three ships?

5. If a 1,027-foot-long modern ocean liner were tied up next to Columbus's three ships, how much longer would it be than the combined length of the *Pinta*, the *Niña*, and the *Santa Maria*?

Kinesthetic Activity

Students dramatize Columbus's arrival in the Caribbean. They assume the roles of Columbus, his companions, and the Arawak people who greeted them. Include as much dialog as possible to emphasize the roles that the different stakeholders played.

Visual–Spatial Activity

Students create a large map of the world for a classroom or hallway mural. The map can be made from pieces of butcher paper taped together. The easiest way to outline such a map is to tack the paper onto the wall and use an overhead or digital projector to project a map of the world onto the butcher paper. Either students or the teacher can trace the outlines of the continents on the paper.

Students can color in whatever features the teacher selects: mountain ranges, countries, rivers, cities, sites of important historical events, homelands of students in the class or of their ancestors, as well as the trajectory of Columbus's voyage. The map can serve as a working document with additional features added as new units are undertaken. The voyages of Columbus and other explorers can also be marked with yarn of different colors. Such a map can grow over the entire school year as new people and places are studied.

Musical Activity

Students listen to period music from European and Caribbean cultures. Most European music in the late fifteenth and early sixteenth centuries was primarily religious. Gregorian chant was still prevalent, madrigals were emerging, and compositions featuring stringed instruments, such as the lute, were popular. (Recordings of such music are readily available.) The music of the Caribbean in the fifteenth and sixteenth centuries is more uncertain. Possibly, however, some of the steel drum music being recorded today is reminiscent of that time and place.

Students listen to the musical selections and reflect on what each piece of music makes them think about, the instruments used in the music and the moods created by each piece of music.

Interpersonal Activity

Working in groups of four to six, students discuss a plan for peacefully blending two cultures. They could address a hypothetical situation between two fictional cultures, between two contemporary cultures, or between the Native American and European cultures being studied.

Some questions the group might consider include:

■ Should one culture take the lead in establishing a blended culture?

■ What separate characteristics of each culture should be retained?

■ What common qualities or features should a new, blended culture develop?

- What should each culture be willing to sacrifice in blending with another?
- How should a form of governance be established?
- How might such blending occur without risking dictatorship?
- Who has the right to decide which elements of each culture should be retained and which discarded?

Intrapersonal Activity

Students respond to the following question in writing: If you had been the chief of the Arawak people, how would you have handled the arrival of the Europeans?

Naturalist Activity

Students study the life forms that live in the Atlantic Ocean and the Caribbean Sea, along Columbus's route. They discuss what marine life Columbus might have observed, how to classify or categorize these creatures by phylum, class, order, etc.

Assessment

Students demonstrate their understanding of the complex issues involved in the arrival of Columbus in America. They draw parallels between two cultures confronting each other today and those of the Native Americans and Europeans in Columbus's time. Students might write or role-play a new family moving into a neighborhood, a new student arriving at a school, or a contemporary international problem. They should address the similarities and differences between the scenario they depict and that of Columbus arriving in the West Indies. They should also anticipate how relationships between converging cultures might unfold.

Lesson 6: Whales

Subject Area: Science

State Standard: Diverse Habitats

Principle Taught: Marine mammals live in water but need to breathe air.

Unit: Mammals

Grade Level: K–8

Materials Needed: library materials on whales, butcher paper and newspaper, song by Judy Collins titled "Whales and Nightingales" or recordings of whale songs, large pieces of colored chalk, book-making supplies

Linguistic Activity

Many books about whales and other aquatic mammals can be found in most school libraries. Depending upon reading levels, students can survey reference books on whales and write brief reports about a variety of whales and how they live in the ocean. For poor readers, the teacher might provide a short lecture with visuals to explain how whales live. Next, students draw a whale, labeling its parts and explaining in both narrative and pictorial forms how whales live and breathe.

Logical–Mathematical Activity

Students explore the lives of whales quantitatively. Fascinating information is available about their size (e.g., blue whales grow up to one hundred feet long), their weight, the amount of food they eat, the temperature of the water in which they live, the depths they dive to, and the lengths of time they can stay under water. Students might create charts comparing and contrasting varieties of whales.

Students could also create story problems using facts about whales. Problems could range from simple arithmetic to more complex problem-solving, as the following examples demonstrate:

1. If five whales meet three whales, how many whales are there?

2. If a whale eats five hundred pounds of krill per day, how many pounds of krill does it eat in a week?

3. If the surface temperature of the ocean is 52° F, and it drops 5°F every seventy-five feet, what will the temperature of the water be if a humpback whale dives to 1,275 feet?

4. Why do beached whales die, when they can still breathe air? (The answer has to do with gravity, lack of buoyancy, and pressure on the lungs.)

Kinesthetic Activity

Many games can be adapted to a whale theme. Whales in the Ocean is one game that can be played outdoors or in the gym. Students line up at one end of the gym or playground. One person is selected as a whale watcher by the teacher. Students are grouped as one of four types of whales (e.g., sperm, humpback, orca, finback). The whale watcher calls out the four types randomly. Students whose whale type has been called run to the opposite end of the playing field. They try to avoid the whale watcher, who tries to tag them. If students are tagged, they, too, become whale watchers. If the original whale watcher calls out "whales in the ocean," everyone runs. The last student tagged becomes the new whale watcher, and the game begins again.

An indoor classroom activity might be the building of a giant whale to hang in the room or hallway. One class I know of made a 25-foot orca by pasting together giant sheets of butcher paper, stuffing the inside with crumpled newspaper, and decorating it. It hung dramatically in the school library for the rest of the year.

Visual–Spatial Activity

To grasp the immense size of a blue whale, students draw one on a paved surface such as a playground, parking lot, or driveway of the school. Using chalk (which washes out with the first rain), a class can quickly sketch and then fill in a large blue whale. Various parts, such as the dorsal fin, blowhole, and baleen, can be drawn and labeled. A second-grade class I know of did just that. The project was featured on the front page of the local newspaper.

For classes inclined to undertake such a project, students can draw to scale the sizes of various whales on individual charts. Most encyclopedias or books about whales provide examples of such charts.

Musical Activity

Several tapes and CDs feature the songs of humpback whales. Some feature just whale sounds while others, such as Judy Collins's album *Whales and Nightingales*, combine whale songs with instrumental music.

Students can analyze this music, listening for specific sounds or patterns. They might listen to it as a focused activity, or the teacher might play it as background music during other classroom activities.

Interpersonal Activity

Combining art, research, and writing skills, students in groups of four or five can make books about whales. The groups divide up the tasks for book making by assigning the roles of researcher, writer, illustrator, layout and binding person, and cover designer. This project will probably require one to two weeks for students to plan, prepare, and construct their groups' whale books.

Intrapersonal Activity

Students write or dictate their own story, answering the prompt, *If I were a whale I would be a* (kind of whale). They should choose a favorite type of whale and write about why they made such a choice. They should address some of the following questions:

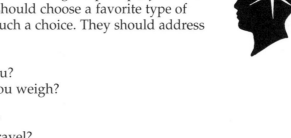

> About how long are you?
> About how much do you weigh?
> What do you eat?
> What do you look like?
> Where do you live or travel?
> How long can you stay under water?
> What is the greatest danger to you?
> How would you feel about living in captivity and being in shows?
> What is unique about the way you live?
> How are you similar to or different from other kinds of whales?
> What are your greatest fears and concerns?

Naturalist Activity

Create a table of whales, including their names and characteristics (e.g., location, length, weight, teeth or baleen, population size, and pod size). This can be done as a whole class, in small groups, or by assigning specific rows or columns to groups or individual students. A suggested template follows:

TYPE	LENGTH	WEIGHT	TEETH OR BALEEN	ESTIMATED POPULATION
humpback				
orca				
minke				
right				
gray				
sperm				

Assessment

The interpersonal or intrapersonal activities in this lesson can be used for assessment.

Lesson 7: Ben Franklin

Subject Area: Social Studies, Civics

State Standard: Democracy

Principle Taught: Freedom of speech is a fundamental American right.

Unit: Colonial America

Grade Level: 4–9

Materials Needed: library materials and Web sites on Ben Franklin, political cartoons, journaling materials

Field Trip (optional): visit to a printing company or local newspaper office

Linguistic Activity

Original source materials are not only more relevant to researchers than textbooks, but are often more interesting to teachers and students, as well. Teachers might want to contact local public libraries or conduct an Internet search, using the keywords *Benjamin Franklin* and *original texts* to find copies of Ben Franklin's original writings. Teachers can use these with students as classroom texts. Some of Franklin's works include *Sayings of Poor Richard*, editions of the *Pennsylvania Gazette*, and his autobiography.

It would be interesting for students to learn that Ben Franklin was not only a statesman and outspoken advocate for democracy but also a successful inventor, writer, political cartoonist, publisher, scientist, diplomat, and gardener. His life itself was a model for freedom of expression, which manifests itself in the form of government Franklin that helped to shape and in which he believed so deeply.

Logical–Mathematical Activity

Ben Franklin was a scientist, inventing many things, such as a wood stove, bifocal glasses, and the lightning rod. He also discovered electricity. Inventing something, he first determined what was needed.

The teacher asks the students to become inventors by identifying a need and then creating something to fill that need. This could be something fantastic—a homework machine or an automatic diaper changer—or something real, such as a 360° fan or new kind of cereal container. In small groups, students should follow these steps to invent something useful:

1. List the needs of one's peers or society.

2. Select one or two needs for the group to engage.

3. Brainstorm a list of possible inventions.

4. Select one invention and one need to address.

5. Create two or more possible designs for the invention.

6. Evaluate the designs and select the best one.

7. Design an invention on paper, with clay, or with other materials.

8. If possible, build a model or prototype.

9. Present the invention the rest of the class and explain how it addresses a need.

One important principle in this lesson is brainstorming. Indirectly, it relates to the concept of free speech. As students prepare for this activity, remind them of the rules of brainstorming:

1. Be freewheeling and creative. Anything goes!

2. Don't criticize others' ideas.

3. Write down *everything* that is suggested.

Kinesthetic Activity

Ben was an outspoken advocate for freedom of the press. When he was young, he acquired a printing press and soon published a newspaper. He felt that it was vital to speak up and write about important political issues. The press was Ben Franklin's instrument for sharing his ideas and opinions.

If possible, it would be valuable to arrange a field trip for students to explore how newspapers and printing presses work. Visits to local newspapers, printing companies, or local museums with old presses can show students the mechanics of the mass production of the written word.

After or instead of a field trip, students might do some of their own printing. Young students can make rubber stamps or create block or potato prints. Older ones may want to work with word processing software and a printer to create titles or headlines for class newspaper. (See the interpersonal activity on next page.)

Visual–Spatial Activity

Ben Franklin often included political cartoons in the papers he printed. Students can also draw their own political cartoons, poking fun at things that they find unjust or unnecessary in the school or community. One rule for their political cartoons is that they cannot poke fun at another person in the class. Political cartoons from local newspapers could be brought in as examples.

Musical Activity

Individually, students write facts they have learned about Ben Franklin, one per note card. On the blackboard the teacher writes the refrain included below. The students practice saying or singing the refrain. They then take turns reading from their cards. After two to four cards are read, the whole group joins in with the refrain.

> *Boogie Woogie Ben*
> *With just a quill pen*
> *Helped make America free*
> *For you and you and me.*

Interpersonal Activity

Working either in groups or as a whole class, students create their own newspaper with a title that including a term such as *gazette, examiner, journal, herald, inquirer,* or *times.* The derivation of such terms could be discussed when choosing the titles. The teacher can also emphasize the fact that newspapers are meant to inquire about or examine what is happening or what people think, and to disperse information. Students should understand that the newspaper is a means of sharing diverse perspectives in a democratic society.

Students can be assigned reporters' roles for their newspaper work. It is effective to have students work in pairs. Projects might address any of the following newspaper components:

School news	World news
Advertising	Artwork
Cartoons	Foreign language column
Weather	TV reviews
Editorials	Book reviews
Sports	Movie reviews
Advice columns	

Intrapersonal Activity

Ben Franklin faithfully kept a diary. Using Franklin as a role model, students begin their own journal or diary. Classroom journals can be used in a variety of ways:

- As a diary which is kept confidential or shared with only the teacher

- As a log to document daily reading or other learning experiences

- For creative writing

- For class dictation exercises

- As a teacher–student dialogue, in which the teacher responds to student's writing

- As a student–student dialogue, for which students are paired and respond to each other's writing

- For a short, daily writing assignments

- To record favorite quotes or passages from books

- A combination of any of the above

Naturalist Activity

Ben Franklin was also accomplished as a scientist and a naturalist. He invented things to harness or control nature, like the lightning rod and swim fins. Students can look around the natural world—parks, prairies, or woods—or look at pictures of natural environments, and then suggest what features man could adapt from bugs, birds, fish, trees, etc.

Assessment

Students write a final essay that measures what they have learned about Ben Franklin. The essay might include information about Franklin's life and his scientific, journalistic, and political work. Students can also state what they consider his most significant contributions and why.

A visual assessment tool might require students to make a collage of Ben Franklin's life, depicting the same categories that the essay might treat. The collage could include original drawings, photocopies, magazine pictures, or combinations of illustrations and text.

Lesson 8: *The Story about Ping*

Subject Area: Language Arts

State Standard: Adventures in fiction can reflect real life

Principle Taught: Emotions are universally experienced.

Unit: China

Grade Level: K–4

Materials Needed: A copy of *The Story about Ping* by Marjorie Flack, materials to make a game board (e.g., markers, butcher paper or card stock, dice), and musical instruments or recordings of Chinese music.

Linguistic Activity

Teachers can read *The Story about Ping* or ask students read it themselves. Most second graders will be capable of reading it independently. As a follow-up, students might orally compose their own stories about animals or people getting lost and their subsequent adventures. Sitting in a circle, one student begins with an opening sentence, and others add to it in turn.

Logical–Mathematical Activity

In the story Ping has many relatives. Every evening, when it is time for Ping to return to the boat on which he lives, the ducks are all counted. Such facts in the story leave opportunities for counting activities. The teacher might ask students what they keep track of by counting, what they do when the count comes up short, and how they think counting got started in the first place.

In addition to answering these questions, students could solve math problems derived from the story:

1. If seventeen ducks got off the boat in the morning and only twleve return in the evening, how many ducks are left behind?

2. If there are twelve ducks and only half of them get off the boat, how many remain on the boat?

3. Ping has nine brothers and thirteen sisters. How many ducklings, including Ping, are in his family?

4. If there are four families of ducks, and six ducks are in each family, how many ducks are there altogether?

5. If one family has twenty-three ducks and another family has thirty-two ducks, which family is larger, and by how many ducks?

6. If a duck ran away from its family to live in the wild, what are some of the main problems it might encounter?

7. If someone gave you twenty-five ducks and you were allowed to keep only one, how would you decide which one to keep and what to do with the others?

Kinesthetic Activity

There are several kinesthetic options for this story. Five suggestions follow:

1. It might be possible to have a pet duck visit the classroom. Students could observe its physical features and behavior, hold it, feed it, and learn how to care for it.

2. A field trip might be arranged to a farm, zoo, or wildlife refuge to observe ducks.

3. Students might make ducks out of clay because this is a shape that even young children can fashion with success.

4. The class might make a duck piñata from papier-mâché and put Chinese rice candies or fortune cookies inside.

5. During recess or PE, students play the game Duck, Duck, Goose, a circle game much like Drop the Handkerchief. To play, all students stand in a circle, facing inward. One student ("it") runs around the outside of the circle, saying, "I had a little duck, and it didn't bite you, and it didn't bite you, and it didn't bite you, but it did bite YOU!" Then "it" tags a student on the back, who races "it" around the circle to see who can be the first to reach the empty space left by the tagged child.

Visual–Spatial Activity

Students draw a map of Ping's adventures on the Yangtze River as follows:

1. Begin by drawing, coloring, or painting a river winding across the page.

2. Add boats, wild animals, other people, and experiences of the duck.

3. Fill in the background with grass, trees, houses, mountains, etc.

Musical Activity

The story of "Peter and the Wolf" emerged from Prokofiev's symphonic work. In this activity, students put the story to music in one of two ways. In the first, students create background sound effects to the story while it is being read; in the second, students to play recorded music that fits the story. I have found that a recording of Chinese music—particularly Chinese symphonic music—accompanies the story especially well. Once students become familiar with their sound effects or with the recording, they can musically accompany classmates who either read the book aloud or tell the story from their story maps.

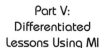

Interpersonal Activity

The teacher makes a board game with a format similar to *Candy Land* or *Snakes and Ladders*. This game would be something like *Rivers and Falls* or the *Yangtze River Game*; each player's gamepiece follows a winding river-path back to a houseboat. Along the way, numerous penalties or rewards await.

A large piece of cardstock or butcher paper serves as the game board. To make the pathway through the game board, tape two markers together and draw parallel lines that wind around the board. This is the river. Next divide the river up into one-inch squares to mark the progress of the players along the board. Then add connecting paths between the stretches of river. These can be waterfalls that students' gamepieces slide down or bridges that advance them upward. Finally, the game board can be embellished in any way the teacher chooses.

Four to six students can play the game at one time, with dice, cards, or a spinner to determine the number of spaces that students each move their pieces in turn. (A circular spinner attached to the game board with a brad eliminates the problem of lost pieces.)

By adding a deck of cards with problems to solve, the teacher adapts the game to incorporate thinking skills and problem solving. Students can also draw cards when they land on previously marked squares, perhaps called Ping squares.

The following are sample problems:

1. Tell the other players how a duck might escape from a mean boy who was trying to catch it, then move your piece forward three spaces.

2. Name one advantage that a duck has over other animals, then move forward one space.

3. State why water pollution is a problem for Ping. If the group approves of your answer, move your piece to the next bridge.

4. Why do you think ducks sleep with their beaks on their backs? Move your piece forward three spaces if you can explain the answer.

5. If one player left this game—the way Ping left his brothers and sisters—how would the departure affect the other players? Talk about this with your group and then move your piece ahead two spaces.

Intrapersonal Activity

The Story about Ping provides a wonderful opportunity for students to discuss something most of them fear and many have experienced—being lost. The teacher can lead a group discussion that addresses what it feels like to be lost, what causes those feelings, the best thing to do when lost, and how to prevent getting lost.

After a brief discussion, students might be asked to illustrate their feelings of fear and happiness.

Naturalist Activity

Using Internet or library resources, students classify different types of ducks, other waterfowl, or birds in general. Categories could include ducks, geese, swans, seabirds, shorebirds, wading birds, and so forth. An Internet search using the keywords *Webster Waterfowl* will lead to useful information for primary students.

Assessment

A simple assessment activity is to ask students to tell the story of Ping to an older student, parent, or other adult. The listener can fill out a brief questionnaire that determines whether the student is capable of relaying key points of the story. For example, questions might include what kind of animal Ping is, where he lives, what happens to him, whether the student adds colorful details to the story, and whether the student tells the story with the proper sequence of events.

Lesson 9: *Animal Farm* by George Orwell

Subject Area: Language Arts and Social Studies

State Standard: Types of Governance

Principle Taught: Totalitarianism is a form of governance.

Unit: Forms of Government and Leadership

Grade Level: 6–12

Materials Needed: copies of *Animal Farm* by George Orwell

Linguistic Activity

Many intermediate and secondary students enjoy George Orwell's *Animal Farm*, an animal fable that satirizes communism. There are several ways that the reading of the story might be approached. A few are below:

1. The teacher reads the story aloud as students follow along in their books.

2. Small groups of students take turns reading the story aloud to each other.

3. Students are assigned portions of the book to read and reflect on in their journals.

After the students have read the story, the teacher might want them to discuss the following key facts from the story:

1. Who are the characters?

2. What is the setting?

3. What do the animals want?

4. What specific course of events lead to the pigs taking charge of the farm?

5. How are the other animals involved in taking over the farm?

6. How does Napoleon rise to power?

7. Once Napoleon takes charge, what control do the other animals actually have over their own lives?

8. Why do the animals continue to believe in Napoleon?

9. What prevents the other animals from challenging Napoleon's power?

10. Do such events happen in human society? Can you provide any examples?

Logical–Mathematical Activity

As an exercise examining cause and effect in the book, students to make a chart showing how the actions of Napoleon and his supporters lead to the downfall of the ideals that the animals had envisioned. Under *Causes*, list Napoleon's actions. Under *Effects*, list the results of his actions. This could lead to a class discussion about whether actions that appear benevolent necessarily are.

Kinesthetic Activity

Many scenes from *Animal Farm* can be dramatized easily. One scene occurs in the barn, when Napoleon first informs the other animals that he is taking charge. This scene could be scripted from the text or simply improvised. Students can be organized into small groups to rehearse their scenes, or the teacher can ask volunteers to improvise the scene just after it has been read.

Visual–Spatial Activity

Students create maps of the farm that include the barns, the farmer's house, the pastures and fields, the site of the windmill, neighboring farms, roads, and the site of the battle. Once students have drawn the maps, they label which events occur where.

Musical Activity

The pigs in *Animal Farm* rely on chants and slogans to indoctrinate fellow animals. Students can recall and list commercial jingles that attempt to sell their products with catchy phrases. Students then create counter-slogans to convince people not to buy these products or to question them.

Interpersonal Activity

Working in groups, students determine their ideal form of classroom or school governance. To begin their brainstorming, they reflect on the following questions:

1. How should leaders be selected?

2. What should be the limits of a leader's power?

3. What rules or laws are most essential?

4. What are the consequences of breaking the rules or laws?

5. How can all students effectively participate in their government?

6. How should they be enforced?

7. Can kids govern themselves? Why or why not?

8. At what age can they be responsible for certain kinds of self-governance?

Each group shares its form of governance with the class. The class could then vote on which, if any, of these components might be used to govern the classroom.

Intrapersonal Activity

In brief essays students respond to the following questions:

1. Which character did you most relate to in *Animal Farm* and why?

2. What form of government do you prefer and why?

3. What role would you want to play in government and why?

Naturalist Activity

Orwell chose pigs as the main characters in the book partly because they are quite intelligent animals. Students think about and write about other animals they consider intelligent, and imagine scenarios or allegories in which their animals assume human qualities. For example, they might consider the significance of their teachers and principal turning into German shepherds or their parents turning into dolphins. They might also contemplate the scenario of having more chimpanzees in the class than children.

Assessment

Teachers collect and review the cause-and-effect charts or the maps that the students have made.

Lesson 10: Harriet Tubman and the Underground Railroad

Subject Area: Social Studies

State Standard: Leadership takes many forms

Principle Taught: Some people find it necessary to take action against social injustice.

Unit: The Civil War

Grade Level: 3–8

Materials Needed: information on Harriet Tubman and the Underground Railroad, maps of the eastern United States, diorama materials (e.g., large pieces of cardboard or cardstock, twigs, colored construction paper, popsicle sticks, etc.), a selection of slave spirituals, and one or more songs from the civil rights movement of the 1960s

Linguistic Activity

Teachers locate information on Harriet Tubman. Several Web sites, biographies and encyclopedic entries are available, and many basal readers contain stories about her. Teachers can learn about Harriet Tubman's life and accomplishments, and share their findings with students in the form of a story. After the storytelling is completed, a discussion of slavery, freedom, and injustice might follow, with the teacher encouraging students to think about the right course of action in an unjust situation.

Logical–Mathematical Activity

The teacher uses story problems to help students understand Harriet Tubman's accomplishments. Depending on the grade level of the students, the story problems might invoule addition, subtraction, multiplication, division, or decimals and percentages. Some examples follow:

1. Harriet Tubman made nineteen trips on the Underground Railroad. She took about sixteen slaves on each trip. How many slaves did she bring to freedom altogether?

2. If Harriet brought twenty-eight slaves to freedom in 1850 and twenty-seven slaves in 1851, how many slaves did she save during those two years?

3. If there were 2,800 slaves in Maryland and Harriet Tubman saved 300 of them, what percentage of the slaves in Maryland did she rescue?

4. If Tubman had to hide forty-two of her companions under a load of straw on a wagon and only seven of them fit in one wagon, how many trips did the wagon have to make to hide all the people?

5. If you were helping Harriet Tubman lead fifteen slaves to freedom and you came to a bridge with a guard on either end, how would you get the slaves across the bridge without getting caught?

Kinesthetic Activity

Working in small groups, students can make dioramas depicting scenes along the Underground Railroad. Before they start working, each group should decide and explain what portion of the Underground Railroad they will create, to avoid duplication among the dioramas.

Visual–Spatial Activity

On a blank map of the eastern United States, students identify various points of the Underground Railroad, noting states, cities, towns, and hiding places along the route.

Musical Activity

There are many old spirituals that the slaves sang on their route to the North. Students learn one of these songs. A brief list of these songs follows:

"Do, Lord"

"Go Tell It On the Mountain"

"He's Got the Whole World"

"I'm Gonna Do What the Spirit Says"

"Jacob's Ladder"

"Joshua Fought the Battle of Jericho"

"Nobody Knows the Trouble I've Seen"

"Old-Time Religion"

"Rock-a My Soul"

"Steal Away"

"Swing Low, Sweet Chariot"

Additionally, songs like the ones listed below emerged during the American civil rights movement in the 1960s and came from or referred back to the time of Harriet Tubman. (In 1977 Walter Robinson wrote a song entitled "Harriet Tubman.")

"Amen"	"Harriet Tubman"
"I'm On My Way"	"John Brown's Body"
"Michael Row"	"We Shall Overcome"
"This Little Light"	

Students can learn one or more songs from each era, and compare and contrast the lyrics. (All the above songs can be found in *Rise Up Singing* by Peter Blood-Patterson.)

Interpersonal Activity

Harriet Tubman courageously took action against social injustice. Her life can serve as a model for students, inspiring them to become aware of such issues as homelessness, poverty, medical care, and abuse.

Students discuss problems in their community to determine whether there is one they would like to tackle. They can then develop a realistic plan to address the problem and start work on their own Harriet Tubman community service project. Some of the service projects I have done with my students include conducting food drives, visiting retirement homes, cleaning local parks, and collecting pennies for UNICEF.

Intrapersonal Activity

When considering important social problems, students can discuss the values that are most important to them, such as altruism, compassion, courage, generosity, kindness, helpfulness, and tolerance. In their journals students can select one value, define it, and reflect on how to express that value in their lives. Students' reflections might lead to a bulletin board on values, letters to the editor of a local newspaper, or a class book of values.

Naturalist Activity

If there is access to a wooded (or other natural) area near the school, the teacher can have students create a map of the woods that references natural features (trees, rock outcroppings, etc.) as a route for someone fleeing injustice. If no such access is available, students can bring branches, small rocks, dirt, and leaves into the classroom and build small dioramas with "secret pathways" and hiding places.

Assessment

For the teacher to assess students' knowledge about Harriet Tubman and her accomplishments, students describe her ideals and beliefs and how she implemented them. This could be written or otherwise. As an alternative, teachers might suggest that students write song lyrics that include this information. Students can also explain what distinguishes someone like Harriet Tubman from other people who may hold similar beliefs but do not act upon them.

Lesson 11: Weather

Subject Area: Science

State Standard: Weather affects people's lives in many ways

Principle Taught: Humans anticipate weather patterns.

Unit: Earth's Atmosphere and Climate

Grade Level: 3–8

Materials Needed: copies of newspapers or access to weather Web site, outdoor thermometer, weather-themed music (e.g., Vivaldi's *The Four Seasons* or Grofé's *Grand Canyon Suite*), photocopies of the following visual-spatial, interpersonal, and intrapersonal activities for all students

Linguistic Activity

Provide students with copies of newspapers. It would be worthwhile to have newspapers from a variety of climates and geographical regions, as well as from different times of the year. The students read articles on weather and its effects and then discuss how weather affects people and how people adapt to various weather conditions. The teacher might list students' responses on the board or on a large piece of butcher paper and post it in the classroom.

Logical–Mathematical Activity

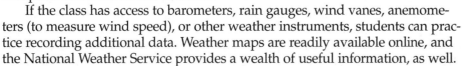

The teacher places an outdoor thermometer near a classroom window or other location where students can check it readily. Students take turns recording daily and hourly temperatures over an extended period of time, and all students maintain a chart of the changes. On the same chart, they can also state how weather affects what people wear and do. After they have kept their charts for several weeks, they can use it to make generalizations and predictions about the weather.

If the class has access to barometers, rain gauges, wind vanes, anemometers (to measure wind speed), or other weather instruments, students can practice recording additional data. Weather maps are readily available online, and the National Weather Service provides a wealth of useful information, as well.

Kinesthetic Activity

Younger students pantomime how people respond to different types of weather. Using an open space, the teacher gives verbal cues:

- Show with your body how you feel when it is hotter than 100°F.

- Show how you feel on a cold, snowy day.

- How do you move on ice?

- How would you move if a hurricane were blowing?

- How would you act after a hurricane had passed?

- Show how would you feel if you heard it was going to rain the day before a class picnic or outdoor field trip.

- Show how you would move in a thick fog.

- Show what you would do if you went outside and found two feet of snow on the ground.

After practicing movements for various types of weather, students can, working in small groups, create their own pantomimes for the rest of the class. These short skits can depict clothing, movement, activities, and reactions to various types of weather.

Older students work in small groups to produce "televised" weather forecasts. Each group member should assume a role, such as statistician, illustrator, announcer, script writer, meteorological expert, camera person, and producer. Students use real data that incorporates the four elements of weather (temperature, air pressure, wind, and moisture), as well as accurate visuals. Students also specify how people will respond to the various weather patterns.

Visual–Spatial Activity

Students draw individual pictures that illustrate the four main elements of weather: temperature, air pressure, wind, and moisture.

Students could also be asked to illustrate other weather phenomena: the water cycle, global wind patterns, movements of air masses (as shown on TV weather reports) the formation of warm and cold fronts, how geographical features affect weather, different kinds of storms, or weather maps that show high and low temperatures in different states or countries.

Musical Activity

Students can listen to Vivaldi's *The Four Seasons* or Ferde Grofé's *The Grand Canyon Suite*, both of which depict different types of weather. Students can listen to entire compositions or selected movements to determine how the composers created the sounds and moods for various types of weather.

Interpersonal Activity

Students usually enjoy scavenger hunts; the following activity introduces them to weather vocabulary. The teacher divides students into groups of four to five, provides each group with a list of weather terms, and informs them that they must find the meanings of as many of the words as possible within a twenty-four-hour period. They must also describe the impact of any of these weather phenomena on people. Students can look up the terms, ask other people, or call the library or local experts at a nearby university. Students must also devise a plan for working together efficiently before they begin.

Before students begin seeking their definitions, it may be wise to have them first discuss what constitutes a good definition. The teacher might give students examples of what is and is not an effective definition. They can practice making their own definitions and should be directed to paraphrase (not copy) the definitions of weather terms. Weather terms for the scavenger hunt follow:

air	humidity	squall
air pressure	hurricane	storm
barometer	hygrometer	temperature
blizzard	ice	thermometer
chinook	jet stream	thunder cloud

lightning	tornado	cloudburst
monsoon	trade wind	cold front
northern	typhoon	cyclone
hail	snow	dew
rain	warm front	vapor
doldrums	rainbow	waterspout
drought	rain gauge	weather balloon
dust storm	sandstorm	weather vane
fog	sirocco	whirlwind
frost	sleet	wind

Intrapersonal Activity

Students to reflect on weather with the following questions and explain why they give the responses they do.

1. What is your favorite type of weather?

2. What is your least favorite type of weather?

3. If you had to choose between living in a very, very hot place and a very, very cold place, which would you choose?

4. How do rainy days make you feel?

5. How do sunny days make you feel?

6. How do snowy days make you feel?

7. How do storms make you feel?

8. How does wind make you feel?

9. If you compared yourself to one kind of weather, what would it be and why?

10. If you could be one of the four main components of weather, which would it be and why?

11. Scientists have developed a large plastic dome that is airtight and contains controlled weather. It has living quarters, gardens, and recreational areas. People have lived in it for up to two years. Would you choose to live in an environment where the weather was completely controlled, or would you prefer to have the uncertainly of normal weather? Why?

Naturalist Activity

The logical–mathematical activity incorporates the naturalist intelligence. The use of weather maps or other data available at the National Weather Service Web site or weather.com can be used for the naturalist activity. As a personalized naturalist activity, students keep a personal weather journal, recording their own observations about the weather on a daily or weekly basis. They could include comments about how the weather affects their moods and temperaments as it changes.

Assessment

Students illustrate the meanings of several weather terms from the scavenger hunt.

Lesson 12: Spring

Subject Area: Language Arts

State Standard: Each season has unique characteristics

Principle Taught: Life is continually changing.

Unit: Seasons and Why They Happen

Grade Level: 3–6

Materials Needed: Ezra Jack Keats's book, *In a Spring Garden*; star charts; seeds and paper cups, or garden supplies; raisins and toothpicks; photocopies of musical and intrapersonal activities

Linguistic Activity

Following a walk outside to observe signs of spring, students read Ezra Jack Keats's book *In a Spring Garden* and other poems about spring. Provide students with an opening line from a poem about spring and ask them to finish the poem on their own. Each student should write at least one or more poems about spring (or any other season). The teacher bind all the student-written poems in a class book, after the students have written and read them. Students can vote on a title for the class's book of poems.

Logical–Mathematical Activity

Several quantitative activities can focus on spring. Students count the hours and minutes of daylight. They can gather the data from an almanac or the daily paper, which provides exact times. Students calculate how much longer each day is than previous ones and keep track for several days or weeks.

Students can also measure the growth of new shoots, branches, or plants; or grow beans, pumpkins, or sunflowers in cups and measure their daily growth. (Even grass can be measured on a daily basis.)

Another possibility is for students to contrast spring in the Northern and Southern Hemispheres, or spring at the North and South Poles. Students might research and explain how the seasons change on Earth. Some may want to make small models to illustrate this phenomenon.

Kinesthetic Activity

Students remake their classroom into a beautiful spring garden. They can try growing mung bean sprouts for snacks, or any other kind of garden vegetables or flowers in paper cups. (One packet of seeds will be enough for the whole class.) Sweet potatoes, carrots, parsnips, or other root vegetables are also attractive plants; students can simply cut off the roots about an inch below the top of them and place the plants in dishes of water. (Avocado pits grow into tiny trees when half-submerged in water, the pointed end facing up.) The plants will grow new shoots in a few days.

If the school has outdoor garden space, the teacher might inquire about whether someone can till a patch of soil for a class garden. If this is possible, students can plan the garden by creating a budget, planning the arrangement of the crops, and planting the garden. (Students in one school in south-central Los Angeles actually turned their garden into a profitable business, creating a fund for college scholarships.)

Visual–Spatial Activity

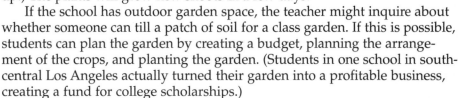

The teacher provides students with charts of the constellations, identifying those that appear in the spring sky. Have students select one or two constellations to make with raisins and toothpicks. Students research facts about the constellations they make.

Musical Activity

Share William Blake's poem "Spring" with students:

> **Spring**
> Sound the Flute!
> Now it's mute.
> Birds delight
> Day and Night;
> Nightingale
> In the dale,

Lark in Sky,
Merrily,
Merrily, Merrily to welcome in the Year.

Little Boy
Full of joy;
Little girl,
Sweet and small;
Cock does crow,
So do you;
Merry voice,
Infant noise,
Merrily, Merrily to welcome in the Year.

Little Lamb,
Here I am;
Come and lick
My white neck;
Let me pull
Your soft Wool;
Let me kiss
Your soft face:
Merrily, Merrily, we welcome in the Year.

Students change the refrain to "Merrily, Merrily, we welcome in the spring." Students then write their own single-phrase descriptors of spring. The class strings the phrases together in verses of five or six lines, with the new refrain inserted at the end of each verse.

This provides the class with a spring song for choral reading. Each student can read his or her lines as they appear in the newly composed song. At the end of each verse, the entire class recites the refrain. It will sound rhythmical and can be further enhanced by creating a melody for the refrain. The song can be adapted for other seasons, as well.

Interpersonal Activity

Organize students into groups. Each group chooses one country or geographical region to study. Using online sources, encyclopedias, social studies texts, interviews with individuals from diverse cultures, or other resources, each group studies how spring is celebrated in another culture or region. Although many modern cultures do not celebrate spring itself, but most have some form of religious, traditional, or even political festival during the spring. Easter, May Day, and ancient Celtic equinox celebrations are examples of springtime rites. When their research is complete, the groups present what they learn to the rest of the class.

Intrapersonal Activity

The teacher leads students in discussion about the changes that each season brings. Students compare such changes in nature to changes within themselves. The discussion might focus on the following question: Seasons change, how have you changed, and how will you change in the future? Students can then write poetic responses, using the following prompts:

Before I was _____

Now I am _____

Next I will be _____
Before I was _____
Now I am _____
Next I will be _____
Before I was _____
Now I am _____
Next I will be _____
And the way I will always remain the same is _____

Naturalist Activity

Again, students could keep a personal record or journal of the changes they see happening as spring unfolds and of their own reflections about those changes. This could be either written or pictorial. Student should use all their senses in their depictions: what new sounds they hear, what smells, what is changing when they look out the window or walk to school. They can also pick a specific location from which to observe these changes: a courtyard, a backyard, the school field, or a park. This record or journal can be revisited with each change in the seasons.

Assessment

Students make a collage of pictures and words about spring. The pictures can be drawn or cut from old magazines or seed catalogs. The collage should depict at least ten characteristics of spring, such as flowers blooming, frogs croaking, birds hatching, days getting longer, spring constellations becoming visible in the Northern Hemisphere, and the occurrence of holidays or festivals around the world.

Lesson 13: Pi, Relationship between Circumference and Diameter

Subject Area: Math

State Standard: Relationships within Geometric Shapes

Principle Taught: Pi is the relationship between the circumference and the diameter of a circle.

Unit: Measurement

Grade Level: 5–12

Materials Needed: information about circumference and diameter, photocopies of the math problems from the logical–mathematical activity, the song from the musical activity, the quote from the intra-personal activity for each student, large pieces of twine for each pair of students, protractors, rulers, compasses, circle templates, scissors, colored paper, simple musical instruments, one eight- or ten-inch paper circle for each student

Linguistic Activity

To introduce students to the concept of Pi, the teacher can make a presentation about the relationship between circumference and diameter or ask students to read a fact sheet that contains such information. The fact sheet can be taken from a textbook, Web site, or an encyclopedic entry. After students have read the information, they write a three-line verse about circles, diameters, and circumference.

Logical–Mathematical Activity

Using the formulas for determining diameter and circumference, students can solve problems, such as the following. (This sheet has been written to photocopy for students.)

$$\text{Circumference} = \pi d \qquad \text{Area} = \pi r^2$$

Circle Math

1. The radius of a circle is 5 centimeters (cm).

   a. What is the circumference of the circle? _____

   b. What is the area of the circle? _____

2. The radius of a circle is 12 cm.

   a. What is the circumference of the circle? _____

   b. What is the area of the circle? _____

3. The diameter of a circle is 43 meters (m).

   a. What is the circumference of the circle? _____

   b. What is the area of the circle? _____

4. The diameter of a circle is 15 miles.

   a. What is the circumference of the circle? _____

   b. What is the area of the circle? _____

5. The area of a circle is 452.16 square centimeters.

   a. What is the radius of the circle? _____

   b. What is the circumference of the circle? _____

When you have finished these problems, you can make up problems of your own using the above formulas.

Kinesthetic Activity

The teacher should remind students that the circumference of a circle is always just a little more than three times its diameters, no matter the size of the circle.

Students work in pairs or small groups. One student at a time forms a circle with her arms. Another student, who has a piece of twine, measures the diameter and circumference of the classmate's circle, determining the relationship between the two measurements. Students should try at least three different sizes of circles to confirm that the relationship between diameter and circumference is constant. To extend the activity, students invent another way to demonstrate this relationship kinesthetically.

Visual–Spatial Activity

Using compasses, protractors, circle templates, colored paper, scissors, and rulers, students create artistic compositions that include only circles and straight lines. Students should be told that the circles can be any size but that the straight lines must be the same length as the circumferences, diameters, or radii of the circles. (Remember: the circumference is always about three times the diameter of a circle.).

Musical Activity

Provide students with some simple instruments and have them create musical accompaniment for the following song.

> **A Circular Song**
> We use circles every day.
> They help us ride our bikes away.
> We see circles through a round eye.
> And we know 3.14 is Pi.
>
> Diameters cut circles in two.
> To get circumference, here's what you do:
> Multiply the diameter by 3.14.
> Now wasn't that an easy chore?

Singing in rounds is an additional musical activity that allows students to experience circularity would be. A list of rounds is included here. With three groups singing the parts to each round several times through, students should begin to see how even music can move in circles.

"O, How Lovely is the Evening"

"One Bottle of Pop"

"Scotland's Burning"

"Kookaburra"

"Make New Friends"

"Hey, Ho, Nobody Home"

"I Love the Flowers"

"Come Follow"

"Row, Row, Row Your Boat"

"Jubilate"

"Happiness Runs in a Circular Motion"

Interpersonal Activity

Students work in pairs. Each student is provided with a paper circle 8" to 10" in diameter. One person in each pair is the reader; the other is the folder. The folder takes a paper circle. The reader reads the following directions as the folder acts on them:

1. Fold the circle in half and crease along the diameter.

2. Fold the circle in half again, forming two perpendicular radii.

3. Unfold the paper.

4. Using the endpoints of two adjacent diameter lines, fold in the flap connecting them, thus forming a side.

5. Repeat the same action with the three remaining sides.

6. What shape do you have?

7. What is the relationship of the length of each side to the circle?

8. Next the partners switch roles. After completing this exercise, students can work together to see how many other shapes they can make with the original circle. Can they make triangles, octagons, or trapezoids?

Intrapersonal Activity

Provide students with copies of the following:

Excerpt from Ralph Waldo Emerson's essay "Circles"

The life of a man is a self-evolving circle, which, from a ring imperceptibly small, rushes on all sides outwards to new and larger circles, and that without end. The extent to which this generation of circles, wheel without wheel, will go, depends on the force or truth of the individual soul. For it is the inert effort of each thought, having formed itself into a circular way of circumstance, . . . to heap itself on that ridge, and to solidify, and hem in the life. But if the soul is quick and strong, it bursts over that boundary on all sides, and expands another orbit on the great deep, which also runs up into a high wave, with attempt again to stop and to bind. But the heart refuses to be imprisoned; in its first and narrowest pulse it already tends outward with a vast force, and to immense and innumerable expansions.

When they have finished the excerpt, students reflect on what they have read, using the following questions and discussing their thoughts with a partner.

1. According to Emerson, how are our lives circular?

2. How do we move from one circle in our lives to the next?

3. Do our circles overlap with each other's?

4. Are there family circles, group circles, national circles, circles of civilization or human evolution?

If the passage is too difficult for students, the teacher can present more simplistically the concept of one's life metaphorically expanding outward like a circle.

Naturalist Activity

Have students look for circles in nature: the sun, moon, rocks, cross sections of branches or trees, ripples in a pond, rain drops, bugs' eyes, tornadoes, gopher holes, etc. Discuss why these circles occur naturally and whether there are advantages or disadvantages of circles or other shapes in nature. In other words, why are these not triangular, square, etc.?

Assessment

Students demonstrate their understanding of Pi by solving problems in the logical–mathematical or kinesthetic activities.

Lesson 14: Comets

Subject Area: Science (Astronomy)

State Standard: Comets are objects that orbit the sun

Principle Taught: The universe is filled with fascinating objects.

Unit: The Solar System

Grade Level: 4–9

Materials Needed: photocopies of the linguistic, musical, mathematical, intrapersonal, and assessment activities below; marshmallows (or, if unavailable, crumpled pieces of paper); soda straws or short sticks (even toothpicks); curling ribbon (or yarn or string); science books; graph paper with small squares; cardstock; rulers; scissors; blue construction paper; white glue in squeeze bottles; glitter (gold, silver, or multicolored) or other art materials; percussion instruments (from the music room or homemade)

Linguistic Activity

Teachers can provide a brief lecture on comets or ask students to read information from their science books or the fact sheet provided on the next page:

Comet Fact Sheet

Comets look like fuzzy stars with tails. They are balls of ice, gas, and dust. Comets travel through the solar system along egg-shaped orbits called ellipses. All comets circle the sun because they are locked into the sun's gravitational field just like planets are. Some comets have short orbits and can circle the sun in a matter of months. Others have long orbits, requiring several hundred years to circle the sun.

The long, shiny tails of comets develop as they draw near to the sun and some tails may stretch over 100 million miles in length. As a comet approaches the sun, the heat causes the icy nucleus to evaporate and to form what is called a coma around the nucleus. The pressure of the sun's light then pushes the small particles of dust away from the coma, forming the tail. A comet's light comes indirectly from the sun. What is visible to viewers on Earth is the reflection of sunlight off the coma and tail of a comet.

The tail of a comet always points away from the sun, causing the tail to trail behind the comet as it approaches the sun. However, after circling the sun and beginning the outward journey in its elongated orbit, the tail actually leads the nucleus of the comet.

One of the most famous comets is Halley's Comet, which is visible from Earth about once every seventy-seven years. It was last visible from Earth in 1986 as it crossed through Earth's orbit.

After students have read the fact sheet, they can respond in writing to the following questions:

1. What words describe the shape of a comet's orbit? [ellipse, cigar, etc.]

2. What is the center of the ball of a comet called? [nucleus]

3. What is the name of the hazy cloud surrounding the center of the ball? [coma]

4. What causes a comet to have a tail? [pressure of the sun's light]

5. Name one famous comet. [Halley's Comet, Hale-Bopp, Swift-Tuttle, Hyakutake]

6. When does the tail of a comet lead? [as the comet travels away from the sun]

7. What are comets made of? [ice, gas, dust]

8. How are comets similar to planets? [They orbit the sun.]

9. How are comets different from planets? [Their orbits are more elongated; they have tails.]

10. Why do you think comets have such strange orbits? [answers may vary; e.g., perhaps because they form at the furthest edge of the solar system]

Logical–Mathematical Activity

Students calculate and draw the tails of different-sized comets on graph paper. Some sample problems follow:

Comet Math

1. Draw a small comet. Then draw a tail that is 5 cm. long.

2. Draw a comet. Then draw a tail that is 15 cm. long.

3. Draw a comet. Then draw a tail that is 25 cm. long.

4. Draw a comet. Then draw a tail that is 2 in. long.

5. Draw a comet. Then draw a tail that is 5 in. long.

6. Draw a comet to fill one square of the graph paper. Draw a tail five times the length of the comet.

7. Draw a comet to fill one square of the graph paper. Draw a tail ten times the length of the comet.

8. Draw a comet to fill one square of the graph paper. Draw a tail twenty-two times the length of the comet.

9. Draw a comet to fill one square of the graph paper. Then find a way to draw a tail fifty times the length of the comet.

10. Draw a comet to fill one square of the graph paper. Then find a way to draw a tail one hundred times the length of the comet.

Kinesthetic Activity

Suggest that students construct their own comets from marshmallows or Styrofoam balls, drinking straws or small sticks, and ribbon or streamers (see illustration on the next page). By carrying their handmade comets, they can simulate the orbit of a real comet by walking around "the sun" and point their comets' tails away from it. The sun can be one student, a big ball, a piece of furniture, or a fan or hair dryer that blows the tail away from the nucleus.

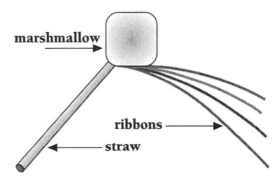

marshmallow

ribbons

straw

Visual–Spatial Activity

Students create a visual of a comet with the nucleus, coma, and tail properly labeled. The teacher provides them with construction paper and art supplies, and suggest that their comets can be drawn, painted, made with glue and glitter, colored sticky-dots and yarn, or other art materials. The example below could easily be made with white glue and glitter. This can also be done on the computer using graphics software.

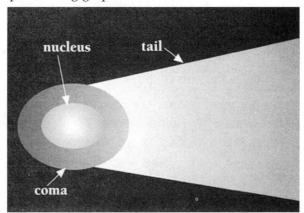

nucleus   tail

coma

Musical Activity

In small groups, students write stanzas of six lines to add to the following song. Each group can teach the rest of the class their lyrics. The melody for this song is "Twinkle, Twinkle Little Star." Students can also accompany the singing with percussion instruments from the music room or homemade ones, such as sandpaper, jars with beans for shakers, rhythm sticks, and large nails. To keep the noise level down, soft percussion instruments—bean bags, Styrofoam, small sticks, and shakers with raisins or small marshmallows inside should be used.

> **A Comet Song**
> Comet, comet, up so high,
> A fuzzy streak across the sky.
> A ball of ice and dust and gas,
> A tail behind you as you pass.
> Comet, comet, as you burn,
> We will wait for your return.
>
> Comet, comet, up so high,
> Streaking back across the sky.
> A ball of ice and dust and gas,
> Your tail before you as you pass.

Comet, comet, far away,
Please come back again some day.

Interpersonal Activity

In small groups, students make one fact puzzle about comets. A fact puzzle requires a sheet of cardstock (or construction paper), 8" x 11" or larger. Each person in the group should make at least one piece of the puzzle. Students begin by writing *comets* in the center of the cardstock. They then draw wavy lines to the edges of the paper to define the pieces. Before cutting out any puzzle piece, students should color the back side of the puzzle to distinguish front from back. Next, they cut out their pieces, with each students each writing comet facts on their pieces. One at a time, students take turns putting together their group's puzzle and those of other groups. As students fit the puzzles together, the teacher asks them to take time to learn and reflect on the factual information the puzzle displays.

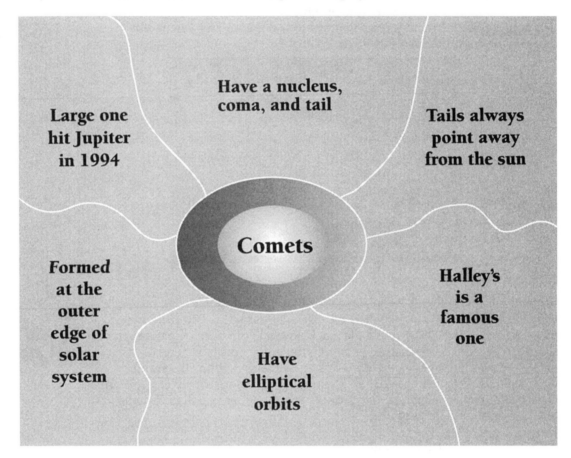

Another option is for small groups to make a comet puzzle, a planet puzzle, a meteor puzzle, an asteroid puzzle, a moon puzzle (etc.) respectively. If each group uses the same template, then an extra challenge is introduced: all puzzles are the same, so a piece from one exactly matches a piece from all the others. If the pieces are all mixed together, the students must sort and categorize them before putting together the puzzles. This task forces students to apply their knowledge of heavenly bodies further.

Intrapersonal Activity

Students discuss with a partner or write their answers individually on the following worksheet:

Comet Questions for Consideration

Name: _____

1. If you were to take a long journey into space to explore distant comets, list ten things you would want to take with you.

2. If you were to be gone for ten years on this journey, what feelings do you think you would have before leaving?

3. How would you share your feelings and with whom?

4. In what ways do you think you might change during the time you are gone?

5. The orbit of a comet is cyclical—that is, the comet passes the same points of its orbit at regular intervals. What are some things in your life that happen at regular intervals? (daily, weekly, monthly, yearly, or even less frequently)

6. Do you like things in your life to happen at regular intervals, or do you prefer unexpected, spontaneous things to happen? Why?

Naturalist Activity

Students create a table featuring comets and their data, then draw conclusions on their own or discuss the data with other students. Similar data can be found by doing an Internet search, using the keyword *comet*.

NAME OF COMET	YEAR DISCOVERED	YEARS TO ORBIT THE SUN	NEXT OR LAST YEAR TO PASS SUN
Chiron	1997	54	2047
Hale-Bopp	1995	2000	1997
Halley's Comet	?	76	2062
Hyakutake	1996	30,000	31,000
Kohoutek	1973	?	?
Shoemaker-Levy 9	1993		Collided with Jupiter in 1994
McNaught	2007	?	2007

Questions that can be asked about this data include:

1. What was the most recent comet observed?

2. What is the range of time that these comets take to orbit the sun?

3. How old will you be the next time Halley's Comet is visible from Earth?

4. How old would you be if you waited to see Hayakutake again?

Assessment

For the teacher to evaluate students' learning about comets, students each choose one of following options that interests them most.

Write a one-to-two page report about comets. Student uses at least three sources of information, including a title page, a bibliography, and at least one diagram. The report should be typed or written neatly.

Write a song about comets that includes at least five facts and musical accompaniment. Student either uses a melody they already know or create your own.

Conduct a mock interview about comets with an "expert." One student is an interviewer, the other a scientist. They must include five to ten important facts about comets in their interview.

Create a diagram or poster about comets. The poster should include information about the physical structure of comets, their orbits, and how they appear to humans on Earth.

Choose any one of the items above and work on it collaboratively with a friend. If this choice is made, both students should take responsibility for certain parts of the work.

Choose a method of presenting what you have learned about comets. The teacher's approval is required before the student beings this project.

Take a written test. The questions provided for the linguistic activity above could be used as test items.

Lesson 15: The Boston Tea Party

Subject Area: Social Studies

State Standard: Independence

Principle Taught: Might doesn't always make right.

Unit: Causes of the American Revolution

Grade Level: 3–10

Materials Needed: copies of Patrick Henry's Give Me Liberty or Give Me Death speech; butcher paper; cash register tape or sheets of 9" × 18" construction paper; tape; photocopies of visual, interpersonal, intrapersonal, and musical activities

Linguistic Activity

The Boston Tea Party was a turning point in British-colonial relations and is a subject studied in many classrooms. After students have learned the causes of the revolt, they might read Patrick Henry's Give Me Liberty or Give Me Death speech, given in 1775. Students can similarly compose "a call to arms" speech to inspire their fellow citizens to rise up against the British.

The speech must include several good historical reasons for revolt, such as the Stamp Act or the Sugar Act. It also must include at least three good reasons the populace should rebel. The speech should be at least three minutes long, have a greeting at the beginning (such as, "My fellow citizens"), and a strong conclusion, (e.g., "For these reasons, I urge you to follow me now as we take up arms against the British. Rise up my friends. Rebel!")

To present other perspectives, alternative types of speeches could be made, such as a call to peace by the pacifists, a call for resolution of the conflict by mediators, a call to leave our land by Native Americans, or a call to subdue by the British. In each case, the speech must present good reasons the audience should follow the advice of the speaker. These reasons should be based on actual circumstances preceding the Boston Tea Party.

As an extension activity, students could be encouraged to make similar speeches (or to write narratives) about thematically related topics of interest to them. For example, they might make a plea to have no homework.

Logical–Mathematical Activity

Students create a time line of events leading up to the Boston Tea Party. The time line might be drawn vertically on lined paper; in book form, with each page highlighting a different event; in a calendar format; or simply on a "line," as shown in the figure below. Graphics software, such as *Inspiration*, can be used if available.

This example of a time line shows only a few of the many events that led to the American Revolution.

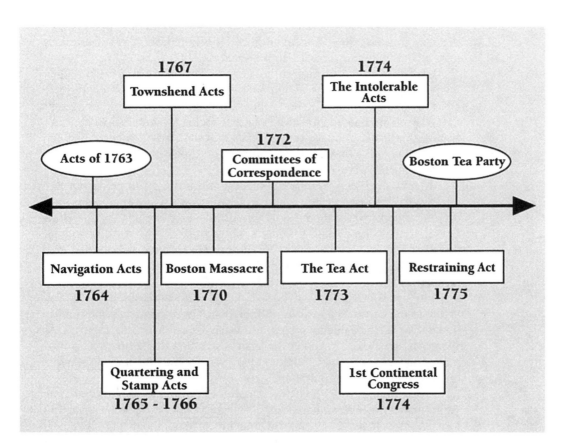

Kinesthetic Activity

The following is a narrative pantomime of the Boston Tea Party, to be read aloud by the teacher while the students pantomime the scene. The only rule is that students cannot touch anyone else during the pantomime. The teacher should practice reading through the narrative ahead of time and, when reading to the class, monitor students' reactions and pause or move ahead as appropriate. Emphasize opportunities for students to use their imaginations to see, smell, hear, and touch the events. It is the senses that will bring the experience to life.

The teacher should also have students participate in a warm-up exercise by asking them to pantomime creeping down a narrow street in the dark, so that no one will see or hear them; climbing up a narrow gangplank onto a ship, twenty feet above the water; dumping a heavy box over the side of a ship without making any noise.

Here follows the teacher's narrative of the Boston Tea Party, which the students pantomime.

You are a young citizen of Boston in 1773. Tonight you are planning a great adventure. To get ready, you have just taken a nap. You are still lying on your bed when you hear the bell on the church steeple ring. You listen carefully. *Twelve* times it rings—midnight. You hear a tapping outside your room. Quickly but very quietly you sit up and pull on your boots. Your hands practically shake with excitement as you lace and tie them.

You stand up and pull on your warm coat as you head for the window. Very carefully, you push the shutters open and climb out, softly touching the ground. Your best friend is waiting for you. With a quick wave to each other you begin sneaking down the dark street together. Cautiously, you peek around the corner. You see other citizens, who were at this afternoon's meeting, also sneaking down the street toward the waterfront. You wave quietly to them and then move back into the shadows.

You creep along the street until you come to a door with a feather hanging on it. You signal to your fiend that this is where you are to meet the others. You tap three times. The door opens and you slip inside. Other citizens like yourself are painting their faces and changing their clothes to look like Native Americans. You take off your coat and slip into a leather shirt. Then you sit down, take off your boots, and put on a pair of leather moccasins. You tie a feather into your hair.

By now everyone is lined up silently at the door. You creep out and begin sneaking down to the wharf. You pass hand signals back and forth to your friends, to let them know when the coast is clear. As you draw closer, you can now smell the salt water of Boston Harbor. You can hear the ships creaking in their berths on the pier. You see the ship loaded with tea, and you crouch down, hiding in the shadows, waiting for the signal to board.

The signal comes and, ever so quietly, watching your balance, you creep up the narrow gangplank onto the boat. Once on board, you quickly find the large crates filled with tea. You wave to your friends to join you. As silently as possible, you open the crates, smelling the strong tea as they open. You pick up the box and dump the loose tea into the harbor. You work hard for several minutes emptying every box.

At last you are done and the signal goes around to retreat. Watching your balance, you creep back down the gangplank. Back on the pier, you turn and watch all of the tea floating in the bay. Silent high-fives pass between you and your friends. Then you return home down the same quiet streets. You climb back in your window, turn and wave good night to your best friend. . . , then quietly close the shutters.

You pull the feather from your head and then lie down in bed and think through the last few hours. What a great adventure! Tomorrow at sunrise, you will return to the hall to get your boots and to talk with your friends. But now, as the church tower strikes two, you slowly drift off to sleep.

Visual–Spatial Activity

Assigned either before or after the narrative pantomime above, a visual assignment might include drawing a map of the route the colonists took from home to the wharf for the Tea Party. The map through Boston could have street names and be turned into a spatial-relations activity, as students give each other directions to follow on their maps. For example: "If you start at the corner of Lexington and A Streets and travel two blocks south and one block west, where will you end up?"

Students could be responsible for drawing their maps, writing their questions, and then checking each other's for correct answers to the questions. This could be done in small groups or pairs. A small-scale example follows:

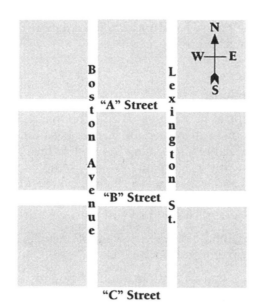

Musical Activity

The following song is to the tune of "Yankee Doodle" and is an easy one for most students to sing, because the majority of them already know the melody. Rhythm sticks, tambourines, and triangles provide good accompaniment. The teacher should provide students with copies of the lyrics or place a copy on an overhead transparency or PowerPoint slide.

> **The Boston Tea Party**
> The War of Independence changed
> the course of history.
> Instead of kings, now people ruled
> with democracy.
>
> The colonies revolted and fought
> England in the war.
> They persevered and formed a nation,
> free forevermore.
>
> It started off one night in Boston,
> Men crept on a boat.
> They dumped the tea into the bay
> And then they watched it float.

The colonies revolted and fought
England in the war.
They persevered and formed a nation,
free forevermore.

Dressed as Indians,
no one knew them
hidden in disguise.
They crept back home triumphantly
with freedom in their eyes.

The colonies revolted and fought
England in the war.
They persevered and formed a nation,
free forevermore.

Interpersonal Activity

Students are in groups of four to five. The teacher hands each group a copy of the card below or of a similar one the teacher has made.

Your group is in charge of planning the Boston Tea Party. Unlike the original planners, you must figure out a way of removing the tea from the ship so it is not wasted. Here are some challenges you will face:

1. There are British guards around so you must be quiet.

2. The gangplank will hold only the weight of one man at a time. It will collapse if he is carrying a load.

3. The tea is in boxes that weigh two hundred pounds each.

4. The sides of the boat are twenty feet above the dock.

The teacher then assigns roles to each member of the group. One person is the recorder. The recorder's job is to write down the approach on which the group decides. Each group's strategy must be written, signed by all group members, and turned in. A second person is the illustrator. This person has to draw a picture or diagram of how the group plans to remove the tea. This document will also be turned in. A third person is the facilitator. This person makes certain that the group sticks to the task at hand and involves everyone in the planning. A fourth person is the speaker. This person will present the group's idea to the whole class, without notes. A fifth person can be the time-keeper, who is responsible for making sure that the group's work is completed in thirty minutes.

To determine roles, students count off within their groups. All ones will be recorders, all twos will be illustrators, and so on. Or each group selects its own roles. If thirty minutes is insufficient, they may use extra time. Groups finishing early can help their speaker practice, color their illustration, or type out their written description on the class computer.

Intrapersonal Activity

Some colonists probably felt confusion about rebelling against the British. Many of them had come from England, and the British had governed most of the colonies for more than one hundred years before the Boston Tea Party.

Suddenly, the colonists had to choose between loyalty to their king and homeland, and freedom and independence. Here is a list of some ideals colonists may have valued:

loyalty	determination
friendliness	freedom
trust	tolerance
courage	justice
patience	faithfulness
kindness	dignity
forgiveness	integrity
peace	responsibility

Undoubtedly, many colonists were uncertain about whether to choose loyalty to England or to pursue freedom. Students can imagine themselves as colonists and make a brief presentation about whether they would choose to rebel, when they had friends and even family who remained loyal to England.

Naturalist Activity

One seldom-mentioned factor that played a role in the Boston Tea Party was the tide in Boston Harbor. As the tide rises, the ships rise higher from view from the wharf or the shore. This played a role in the visibility of the colonists to British guards. Have students consult tide tables to determine the variation of water height (about a twelve-foot differential). Tide tables are available on the Internet (accessed via a search with keywords *tide tables* and *Boston Harbor*) or from the Massachusetts Marine Trade Association.

With copies of a monthly tide table, students can determine which day of the month has the highest tide, which day has the lowest, which has the greatest differential, and when is a good time to go to the beach. Some Web sites have tide charts in graph form, which are easier to read because they show a graph of the tide going up and down each day.

Assessment

Use the students' time lines to assess their understanding of events leading up to the Boston Tea Party.

Lesson 16: *The Search for Delicious* by Natalie Babbitt

Subject Area: Language Arts

State Standard: Resolving Conflict in Literature

Principle Taught: People often assume that their way is the only way to do something.

Unit: Fiction

Grade Level: 3–6

Materials Needed: one or more copies of the book; costume box of old clothes, capes, scarves, burlap bags, etc.; large boxes for background sets; chart from the book for visual activity; photocopies of mathematical and interpersonal activities; twelve- to twenty-four-inch boards; screw eyes; and fishing line (or wire or old guitar strings)

Linguistic Activity

Natalie Babbitt's book *The Search for Delicious* is a wonderful book for intermediate-aged children. It portrays the fictional journey of Vaungaylen, a young boy, through his kingdom, to determine what people consider to be the most delicious food of all. He encounters a number of intriguing characters and situations along the way. The story revolves around interpersonal conflict and how to manage it.

For their linguistic activity, students could read the book if a class set is available. If not, the teacher could read the book aloud. For nonreaders or readers of low ability, a reading of the book could be taped, or others in the class might guide the nonreaders through the book.

As an additional linguistic activity, students might write a character sketch of one of the interesting individuals in the book. Here is a list of characters to choose from:

The Prime Minister	The King	The Queen
Gaylen	Hemlock	The General
The Mayor	The Woldweller	Mrs. Copse
Ardis	Pitshaft	Medley
The Minstrel		

Directions for the students might include writing a one- to two-page description of one of the characters listed on the chalkboard, in which the student tells who the character is, where the character lives, when the character enters the story, why the character is important in the story, and why the student selected that particular character to write about.

Logical–Mathematical Activity

Listed are several logical possibilities for teachers to choose from:

1. Percentages: Students conduct a survey to of the class's favorite candy bars and then calculate the favorites by percentage.

2. Graphing: Students work with the statistics gathered in the first activity to create bar graphs, line graphs, or pie charts. (There are easy-to-use software applications available for this kind of graphing.)

3. Measuring: Students figure distances in Gaylen's journey from scene to scene. Some sample problems are provided.

4. Story problems: See page 113.

1. Gaylen traveled twenty-seven miles from the castle to the first town, eighteen miles from the town to the forest, eleven miles farther to the apple orchard, twenty-nine miles to the Mildews farm, and then back to the apple orchard. How far did he travel?

   _____

2. Gaylen left the dwarf's cave at 1:00 p.m. and traveled for three and one half hours. He stopped for lunch for forty-five minutes, and then he traveled for another two hours and twenty minutes to the third town. What time was it when he arrived?

   _____

3. Gaylen traveled from the castle to the lake, and then to Nest of the Wind fifteen times. The distance between these places was 24 miles. How far did Gaylen travel altogether?

   _____

4. If the entire journey from the castle to the lake was 114 miles, but could be cut short 47 miles by going straight from Mrs. Copse's house to the lake, how far would it be taking the shortcut?

   _____

5. If Gaylen traveled 114 miles from the castle to the lake heading east, and the Prime Minister traveled 66 miles from the castle to the lake heading west, how far was a complete trip around the kingdom?

   _____

6. If Hemlock left the castle on Thursday, April 7 and Gaylen left on Saturday, April 9, and Hemlock arrived at the second village on Tuesday, April 19, but it took Gaylen 5 days longer, when did Gaylen get there?

   _____

7. If Gaylen decided to stay with Mrs. Copse, who lived 76 miles from the castle, and if he wanted to visit the Prime Minister four times a year, how far would he travel back and forth in three years?

   _____

Kinesthetic Activity

The book lends itself naturally to a staged production. There are numerous characters, enough for each person in a class, to portray. There are about five main scenes: the castle, the towns, the forest, the cave, and the lake. Costumes might be minimal or imaginative and ornate.

A script can be written by the teacher, the class as a whole, or by small groups working on different scenes. One excellent technique for developing a script is to have students role-play different scenes in the play, allowing the script to emerge from their impromptu dialogues.

If a major production is not practical, small-group performances of individual scenes can be great fun. Working in groups of four to six, students can easily portray most of the book's major events. Here are some suggestions for scenes:

■ The first argument between the king, queen, Hemlock, and others

■ The Mayor, Medley, and Gaylen in the first town

■ The woldweller scene (Several students could play woldwellers.)

- The scene in the apple orchard (Muzzle and Marrow included)

- The Mildew's farm

- The dwarf's cave

- Ardis and Gaylen at the lake

- Hemlock's scene at the lake

- The final scene at the lake (Paper grocery bags stuffed with newspapers make great "rocks" to stack up for a dam.)

Visual–Spatial Activity

If students plan to dramatize scenes from the book, drawing and painting sets will provide challenging visual activities. Another visual–spatial option is for students to make large picture-story charts of the kingdom and of Gaylen's itinerary. The book contains an illustrated map that can be used as a model. Simply following this map as the story progresses is a good spatial reasoning skill.

Musical Activity

On page 59 of *The Search for Delicious*, the minstrel sings a song to Gaylen while playing the harp. As a musical activity, students can make their own stringed instruments. Simple materials are required: a piece of wood, screw eyes, and fishing line, wire, or old guitar strings. A cigar box or comparable container can be improvised as a resonating chamber. The instrument can be used to accompany the minstrel's song or students' songs. In addition, students who are learning to play real stringed instruments could bring theirs to class and explain the stringing system, as well as how to make different sounds.

To make the stringed instruments, screw two screw eyes halfway into opposite ends of the stick or board. Tie a piece of wire as tightly as possible to each screw eye. Twist the screw eyes in tightly to tune the string. Using strings of different lengths, creates variation in tones, but the best control of the tone is done by tightening the wires. Any type of tub, bucket, or box underneath the strings will help the sound resonate.

Interpersonal Activity

Babbitt's book gives numerous examples of interpersonal conflict. Identifying the story's conflicts provides students with opportunities to reflect on and learn ways to resolve or manage conflict. The castle scene, the town scenes, the farm scenes—even the scene at the lake—could all be handled differently, were the characters willing to negotiate and create win-win outcomes.

A model for conflict negotiation is provided below. Some classes, however, prefer to develop their own strategies, create a written set of procedures, and practice them with classroom conflicts.

Conflict Resolution

While there are many approaches to resolving conflict, most involve the following components:

1. Define exactly what the problem is. It is important to avoid "you" statements (which blame), and instead use "I" statements when defining the problem.

2. Brainstorm a list of possible solutions.

3. Choose the best option.

4. Develop an action plan.

5. Implement the action plan.

6. Reflect on whether or not the solution worked and make revisions as needed.

When students are initially learning conflict-resolution procedures, the teacher should suggest that small groups is more effective than working in large ones. After the students are organized in small groups, the teacher identifies the steps of conflict resolution and posts a chart of the six steps, to which they can later refer. The teacher suggest several conflicts and ask students to practice resolving each. Once students gain familiarity with the process, they can address and attempt to resolve actual classroom problems.

Intrapersonal Activity

The Search for Delicious provides an interesting metaphor for students' personal journeys—trips they have taken, personal adventures they have had, or their own experiences growing up. Students write about such journeys, either in the form of a narrative about their lives or about a single but important incident. Students can also give a fictional account of a search, in which they are each the main characters. The journeys might be described in a pattern similar to that of the book. It is important that the teacher (or the teacher and students together) determine the length of the written work, when it is due, and the writing standards.

Naturalist Activity

In *The Search for Delicious*, Vaungaylen's journey takes him through a forest, a meadow, rocky outcrops, mountains, and streams. For a naturalist activity, students create maps of the kingdom with these various habitats represented pictorially. For instance, the castle could lie at the center of the picture, and Gaylen's journey could be traced through the various environments depicted in the book. Students could identify which plants and animals might live in each part of the kingdom, how the weather might vary from region to region, and where they would prefer to live.

This could be done as a whole class, in small groups, or by students independently. It's a great way not only to investigate the different environments but also to consider the intricacies of mapmaking.

Assessment

Just as the Prime Minister creates dictionaries in the book, students can create individual dictionaries for assessment. One word (or more) for each letter of the alphabet would determine the book's organization. The class might want to choose a general theme for all students' dictionaries to treat, such as ways to resolve conflict, or thoughts about the story itself. Or students might choose their own themes.

Lesson 17: Shape and Change—A Lesson on the Volume of a Cylinder

Subject Area: Math

State Standard: Volume of a Cylinder

Principle Taught: Volume increases as the radius increases.

Unit: Geometric Solids

Grade Level: 2–9

Materials Needed: plain 8.5" x 11" paper; five or six bags of dry cereal; calculators; rulers; tape; and small marshmallows, sand, or any material that can be easily poured into a cylinder

For this lesson, I take a slightly different approach. I still use Multiple Intelligences to differentiate, but I provide less structure and more choice. In other words, students select with which intelligences they prefer to solve the problem.

Preparation

The teacher explains to the class that they will be learning about different shapes and about what happens to different shapes when they are changed. (Tell them that today they will be learning about a shape called a cylinder. Ask whether any of them know anything about cylinders. Gather thoughts from the class.)

The teacher next explains that students will be working in small groups and divides the class into groups of four to six students. The groups each select (or the teacher selects) a recorder in each group. The recorders write down these two questions:

1. How do we figure things out?

2. How are we convinced?

The teacher should tell the recorders that part of their job will be to observe their groups responding to these two questions, and to keep notes.

The teacher hands out a sheet of paper to each student and asks students to take their sheet of paper and roll it into a *cylinder*, the short way. The students bring the edges precisely together, just touching each other. That way everyone will have exactly the same size and shape of cylinder. The teacher asks them to take a minute to explore this cylinder: to look through it, reach through it, talk through it, get to know this cylinder.

The teacher then has the students unroll their cylinders and says, *Now we are going to change the shape and make a new cylinder.* The teacher asks them to roll their papers into new cylinders, the tall way. Again, the teacher asks them to bring the edges precisely together, so everyone's cylinder is of the same size and shape. The teacher again encourages the students to explore their new cylinders.

Last, students unroll their papers again and the teacher asks, "Which of the two cylinders—the short one or the tall one—holds the most stuff?" The teacher invites the students to use any means they choose to answer the question, remind them of the bags of cereal, the calculators, the ruler, the class computer, and any other resources available. The recorders start observing their groups at this point.

The groups can take about ten minutes to come up with an answer. (I usually post the formula for the volume of a cylinder ($V = \pi \times r^2 \times h$) on the board for anyone who asks or who wants to take a mathematical approach.) The teacher then roams the class, handing out tape when needed. The teacher should refrain from answering questions while the students try to answer the question for themselves.

After ten minutes, students wrap up their work and the recorders report to the whole class on the two questions they were to answer (*How did your group figure things out? How were they convinced?*). When they've completed their reports, the teacher can add on any strategies observed but that the recorders did not report. For example, did someone ask for the formula? Did anyone leave the group to see what another group was doing? Did anyone draw pictures? Remind students that they could have done anything they wanted to solve the problem. It will become clear that they used many intelligences to solve this problem. The teacher can even ask the class which intelligences were used after the recorders are done presenting.

Following is an assessment task I made to determine if my students really understood the somewhat counter-intuitive results of this problem. It's called Pick Your Pop.

Pictured on the right are two containers of different sizes for a new kind of pop called Pizzaz. The company wants kids to choose which container they like best. As a consumer, students decide which one they think contains the most pop and explain their answers.

To evaluate the Pick Your Pop assessment task, here is a rubric created by my students and me. Students are evaluated not only for container selection but also for their reasoning. In a differentiated classroom, it is good to evaluate different skills because kids think and learn in different ways, using different intelligences. Points are awarded based on which assessment best describes each student's efforts.

	1 POINT	**2 POINTS**	**3 POINTS**	**4 POINTS**
Container selection	Selection indicates no understanding of relationship between shape and change.	Selection indicates little understanding of relationship between shape and change.	Selection indicates some understanding of relationship between shape and change.	Selection indicates clear understanding of relationship between shape and change.
Explanation of reasoning	Explanation is disorganized and quite illogical.	Explanation is somewhat disorganized and illogical.	Explanation shows some clarity and logic.	Explanation is clear, succinct, and highly logical.

By the way, the correct answer is that the short cylinder actually holds about 25 percent more than the tall one. Intuitively, it seems that they have identical volumes because they both have the same surface area. In fact, the two cylinders don't have the same surface area because the tops and bottoms are part of the surface area, and they are clearly different. The formula gives the mathematical explanation: as height increases, the volume grows gradually, but as the radius increases, the volume grows exponentially. I've done this mostly with fourth and fifth graders, but even my second and third graders have enjoyed it.

Lesson 18: An MI Alphabet

Subject Area: Language Arts

State Standard: Letter Recognition and Beginning Phonics

Principle Taught: Letters make sounds; sounds make words.

Grade Level: Kindergarten

Materials Needed: story and nature books, boxes with pictures, cookie sheets, and magnetic letters

Linguistic Activity

Students read an alphabet book, such as Audrey Wood's *Alphabet Mystery* or *Alphabet Adventure*.

Logical–Mathematical Activity

Students count the number of lines each letter has.

Kinesthetic Activity

Students spell their names on cookie sheets with magnetic letters and say their names aloud.

Visual Activity

Together, students decorate twenty-six small boxes, each with a letter. In each box students then put pictures of items that begin with the respective letters (e.g., the *A* box has pictures of ants and apples).

Musical Activity

Students sing the alphabet song while pointing to each letter and shaping each letter with the their fingers.

Interpersonal Activity

Students work in pairs and take turns working with cookie sheets and magnetic letters forming words that the teacher has written on the board or provided on cards at their tables. If a student asks for help, the partner assists.

Intrapersonal Activity

Students pick their favorite three letters, then draw and say them.

Naturalist Activity

Students identify the letters used to spell the names of animals, insects, plants, or trees.

Assessment

The teacher assesses students' efforts for the intrapersonal activity: How many words did they make? Were they spelled correctly?

Lesson 19: An MI Literature Lesson on Edgar Allan Poe

Subject Area: Language Arts

State Standard: Reading, Analyzing, and Responding to a Literary Genre

Principle Taught: Summarize elements of fiction, identify emotions in a work, and write a piece that evokes similar emotions.

Grade Level: 7–9

Materials Needed: copies of "The Tell-Tale Heart"

Linguistic Activity

In trios, students read and summarize the plot, setting, character, and point of view of "The Tell-Tale Heart." They then discuss Poe's descriptions in the story.

Logical–Mathematical Activity

Trios of students make time lines of the story's plot and of how the point of view of the character evolves.

Kinesthetic Activity

Each trios select one part of the plot to act out.

Visual Activity

Each person in the trios finds or makes visuals that realistically or abstractly represent the plot, character, and setting of the story.

Musical Activity

Students select tapes of background music to enhance specific scenes from the story.

Interpersonal Activity

Trios research Poe's life and character to understand what might have inspired his ominous stories.

Intrapersonal Activity

Trios identify events that evoke fear, insanity, or loneliness. Trios create a written narrative or a dramatization that demonstrates or evokes similar feelings.

Naturalist Activity

Students identify natural environments that evoke feelings such as fear, loneliness, and solitude.

Assessment

Students take a quiz on elements of fiction and their understanding of Poe's story, or the teacher uses a rubric to assess students' original work.

Lesson 20: MI Spelling

Subject Area: Language Arts

State Standard: Spell grade-level words correctly

Principle Taught: Correct spelling is important in writing.

Grade Level: 1–3

Materials Needed: spelling lists, paper, and colored markers

Linguistic Activity

In pairs, students make up a story using all their spelling words. They each tell their stories to their partners, stopping to spell each of the spelling words.

Logical–Mathematical Activity

Students create word categories, for example, words with three, four, five, six letters, or words with more than one vowel, or a list of the words from the shortest to longest.

Visual Activity

Students write words using different colors or sizes for parts of the spellings that they find confusing.

Kinesthetic Activity

Students spell words with their bodies: arms out for *T*s, up for *Y*s, rounded for *U*s, and so on. The teacher can provide background music to which students turn spelling their body-letters and -words into dances.

Musical Activity

Students sing-spell words to a melody, or create rhyming patterns. (e.g., color-bo-bolor-fee-fi-fo-folor—c-o-l-o-r; family-bo-bamily-fee-fi-fo-family—f-a-m-i-l-y; weather-fo-feather- fee-fi-fo-feather—w-e-a-t-h-e-r.)

Interpersonal Activity

In pairs, students use the Think-Pair-Share strategy to practice words.

Intrapersonal Activity

Students set personal goals and timelines for learning their spelling words. For example, they might aim to learn five words on Monday, five words on Tuesday, and so forth.

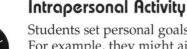

Naturalist Activity

Students practice target words by spelling them out with sticks, tall grass, flower stems, or other natural objects.

Assessment

Students take a spelling test individually.

Lesson Planning Form Using MI
to Differentiate Instruction

For teachers who want to create their own Multiple Intelligences lessons, a sample format should be provided below. The form is enlarged to make it easier to capture all ideas. Copies of these can be inserted into your lesson-plan book or bound together to create an entire book of differentiated lesson plans. Teachers should remember that it is not necessary to include every intelligence in every lesson; in fact, it can be counterproductive to do so. It is important, however, to integrate every intelligence into students' learning over a period of time or throughout a series of lesson plans.

Lesson title: _____

State standards being addressed: _____

Student outcomes: _____

Linguistic activity: _____

Visual–spatial activity: _____

Logical–mathematical activity: _____

Musical activity: _____

Kinesthetic activity: _____

Interpersonal activity: _____

Intrapersonal activity: _____

Naturalist activity: _____

Assessment: _____

Materials and resources needed: _____

Sequence of activities: _____

Part VI

Preparing Students for Self-Directed Learning in a Differentiated Classroom

One of the greatest rewards in Multiple Intelligences teaching has been observing students work in their areas of strength through their independent projects. Many teachers face a dilemma when attempting to integrate Gardner's theory into their classrooms. They wonder whether to emphasize the Multiple Intelligences on a daily basis or whether to nurture individual students' strengths. I choose to do both because the self-directed learning through independent projects is such a powerful way to differentiate instruction.

I dedicate as many as four to five hours per week to student projects. For most projects, students pursue curricular topics in greater depth. This helps me cover the state and district standards in more breadth. Moreover, the choices that students make for their projects frequently reveal their inherent intelligence strengths. Through the projects, students learn how to plan, manage, and bring closure to their self-selected tasks. So often schools emphasize creating autonomous learners—I feel fortunate to have found concrete ways to nurture self-directed learning in my students. Part VI contains strategies to achieve this.

Part VI Contents

123

Part VI: Preparing
Students for Self-
Directed Learning
in a Differentiated
Classroom

How to Organize Independent Projects

When I began differentiating instruction through Multiple Intelligences, I thought the highlight of my program was the MI learning centers. On a daily basis, students approached content and skills in multiple ways. Over the years, however, I have found that the independent-project work is equally valuable. The projects enable students to apply and further develop the concepts and skills they have gained at the centers. While students enjoy their active, center-based learning, they even more eagerly pursue their independent projects. It is the projects that teach my students how to direct their own learning and how to apply the skills and knowledge from the centers.

To organize independent projects, students identify their topics, research them for three to four weeks, plan, prepare, and give demonstrations of what they have learned. At the end of each month, I dedicate two or three afternoons for students' presentations. These are not presentations in which students read or give a memorized talk. Instead, they share their learning through skits, songs, poems, stories, dances, interviews, "game shows," charts, posters, diagrams, graphs, puzzles, problems to solve, videotapes, and interactive group activities.

The presentations are informative and engaging. More importantly, they are empowering to the student researchers. Not only do students develop expertise in their chosen areas, they also gain communication skills while deepening their areas of strength. Following each presentation, classmates compliment and then critique the research and demonstration. My students learn how to give and receive constructive feedback.

All project presentations are videotaped. At the end of the year, each student receives a videotape or CD of that year's projects. The tapes reveal students' growth over time, typically showing improvement in research strategies, content knowledge, and communication skills.

Although I encourage my students to select their own project topics, I will at times collaborate with them to decide what might be an appropriate topic for them to pursue. If I am playing an active role in identifying topics, I try to provide several options, so that students learn to make choices. In addition, I require that the students always determine how they will communicate what they have learned to their classmates and me.

Once the topics are chosen, students complete contracts like the one shown on pages 125–126. The contract helps organize students' work by asking them to identify the steps they will take to complete their work.

Since students are not necessarily self-directed by nature, there are many things a teacher needs to do to help them develop independent learning skills. At the beginning of the school year, I explain that one of the things they will learn is how to conduct independent projects. I tell them that there are "warm-ups" to prepare for this type of learning. These consist of (1) identifying exciting topics, (2) figuring out how and where to get information, and (3) determining how to demonstrate one's learning. The whole class discusses these three warm-ups together and then brainstorms possibilities.

124

Part VI: Preparing
Students for Self-
Directed Learning
in a Differentiated
Classroom

Warming Up to Self-Directed Learning

1. **Identify exciting topics:** It's important to ask students what they most want to know about the content areas we study. While some students initially might not think of a topic, most students quickly identify possibilities. Sometimes just listening to their classmates' ideas encourages them to consider options. However, some students will need the teacher's assistance in selecting topics, and I always provide suggestions.

2. **Figure out where and how to get information:** While many topics are fascinating, I suggest that students select ones that are easily researchable. My students and I also discuss different ways to access information. Students rely on the Internet, book research, printed matter from organizations, interviews with knowledgeable adults, guest speakers in the classroom, newspapers, films or television programs, telecommunications and software, and observations or experiments. Students quickly learn that the process of research can be enjoyable.

3. **Determine how to demonstrate one's learning:** Students are each responsible for teaching the rest of the class what they have learned. I require my students to give multimodal project presentations. Multimodal demonstrations of learning include charts, videotapes, skits, songs, talk shows, drawings, dances, slogans, banners, models, dioramas, sculptures, letters, statistics, quilts, community service efforts, inventions, guest speakers, and videos.

After discussing the three warm-ups, I explain the eight steps to do a project. I hand out photocopies of the eight steps, and the whole class reviews them together. The steps are illustrated with a sample topic.

Eight Steps for Doing Projects

1. **State your goal:** I want to understand how visual illusions work.

2. **Put your goal into the form of a question:** What are visual illusions and how do they fool our eyes?

3. **List at least three sources of information you will use:** Library books on visual illusions, eye doctors or university professors, prints of M. C. Escher's work, and the art teacher.

4. **Describe the steps you will use to achieve your goal:** Ask the librarian to find books on visual illusions, read those books, look up *visual illusion* in the encyclopedia, talk to the art teacher about visual illusions, and look at Escher's work.

5. **List three to five ideas you want to research:** What are visual illusions? How is the human eye tricked? How are visual illusions made? Who are some artists who have made art with visual illusions? Can I learn to make some visual illusions?

6. **List at least three methods you will use to present your project:** Explain what optical illusions are, make a diagram of how the human eye works, make posters with famous optical illusions, try to make optical illusions of my own, hand out a sheet of optical illusions for

class members to keep, and have the class try to make optical illusions of their own.

7. **Organize the project into a timeline:**

Week 1: Read sources of information
        Interview adults
Week 2: Look at a variety of optical illusions
        Try to make my own optical illusions
        Make diagram of eye
        Make handouts for class
Week 3: Practice presentation
        Present to class

8. **Decide how you will evaluate your project:** Practice in front of my parents and get their feedback, practice in front of my best friends and get their feedback, ask class for feedback on my presentation and visuals, fill out self-evaluation form, read teacher's evaluation, and analyze videotape of my presentation.

After the students have discussed the eight steps for doing projects, they are usually ready to write their project contracts. The contracts organize their independent learning and inform the teacher of what students intend to study. I keep the contracts in a file folder on my desk. Because the contracts require that research questions and resources be identified immediately, it becomes evident within a day or so whether a contract is actually viable for a particular student. Sometimes students have to change their topics and, when this happens, they complete new contracts. After the first couple of project efforts, however, students become adept at selecting researchable topics. Following here is the project contract my students complete:

Project Contract

Name: _____   Topic: _____

Research question: _____

_____

List the steps you will take to do this project:

_____

_____

_____

_____

List at least three sources of information you will use:

_____

_____

_____

_____

List at least three big ideas you will research:

_____

_____

_____

_____

_____

_____

List at least three ways you will demonstrate what you have learned:

_____

_____

_____

_____

Target completion date:

_____

Below is the evaluation form I use to assess project work. The form includes three sections: the first is the teacher's written evaluation, the second is where the teacher copies the positive and critical feedback classmates provide orally, and the third section asks for the student's self-assessment. A rubric or scoring scale can also be included.

Project Evaluation Form

Teacher Comments

Research: _____

Information: _____

Organization: _____

Presentation: _____

Other: _____

Peer Comments

_____

_____

_____

Self-Assessment

What did you learn about your topic? _____

What did you learn about presenting? _____

What was the hardest part for you? _____

What was the best part for you? _____

What do you want to learn more about? _____

Differentiating Homework

In some schools, parents and students expect homework to be assigned on a regular basis—even in the primary grades. As a teacher, I attempt to make homework interesting and engaging, hoping that students will want to do their homework, One differentiated approach I've used is assigning students weekly homework in the Multiple Intelligences. Each week, an assignment in one intelligence is sent home for students to complete by Friday. Over a period of several weeks, all of the intelligences are covered and a new rotation begins. Sometimes the homework nicely integrates class content and, at other times, it is independent of our curricular themes.

My students actually look forward to getting their homework each week. Some are excited because this approach lets them all be successful with homework at least some of the time. Students also enjoy the variety of activities, and I appreciate how classroom learning extends into the home and community. Some parents have also told me that they have never witnessed such enthusiasm for learning "after hours."

I list here eight examples of homework assignments that are appropriate for intermediate grade levels and that can easily be adapted for primary or secondary grade levels. In short, I try to teach students learning skills through homework or give them activities that they will enjoy doing outside of class.

The homework samples below are written directly to students and can be photocopied and distributed if desired.

Linguistic Homework

Collect three news items during the week about the same topic, such as a war, an election, or the rescue of someone in distress. If you do not have a newspaper, write down what the Internet, TV or radio news reports about the topic for three days. Compare and contrast what information is shared each day and how different sources, if available, talk about the same event. At the end of the week, be prepared to share with a small group what your topic is and how it has changed throughout the week.

Logical–Mathematical Homework

Your job this week is to hunt for bargains. Look in the newspaper, in the advertisements that come in the mail, in catalogs or coupon books, on TV or radio commercials, or in grocery or other stores.

128

Part VI: Preparing
Students for Self-
Directed Learning
in a Differentiated
Classroom

Find at least ten items that are on sale. List each item with its regular and sale prices. Then list the amount you would save by purchasing each item at its sale price. Record this data on a chart with four columns. At the bottom of the chart, total all of the regular prices, all of the bargain prices, and the total amount saved if you were to purchase all ten (or more) items.

If possible, try to find items that you or your family would actually buy. In this way, you would be helping your family save money.

For extra credit, calculate the percentage markdown for each item. For example, if the regular price of an item is $10.00 but the sale price is $5.00, the markdown is 50 percent. After making all of these calculations, figure the percentage markdown on your total savings.

Kinesthetic Homework

Design and construct a bridge out of toothpicks and glue that is both strong and light. As you plan and build your bridge, keep in mind how the weight is distributed along the structure. Your bridge should provide maximum support to the area where the weight will be applied. Use as many toothpicks and as much glue as you want. The bridge should be able to span 18 cm. It should be no more than 10 cm wide and no more than 24 cm long.

There must be a bridge deck that a toy truck could use to cross the bridge. The truck is 4 cm wide and 5 cm tall. The deck may be at any level of the bridge.

Your goal should be to make the strongest bridge possible. It will be tested for strength in class on Friday. The strongest bridge will win a prize.

Visual–Spatial Homework

Make a "flip-flop" (also called a fortune teller) with eight questions and answers about a topic that we have been studying in school.

- Begin with a square sheet of paper about nine inches by nine inches.

- Fold it in half, then into four square quarters.

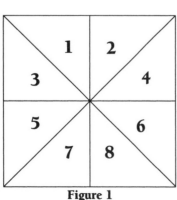

Figure 1

Figure 2

- Unfold it to the original square.

- Fold each of the four corners to the center (Figure 1).

- Turn it over and fold each of the four new corners to the center.

- Fold it in half with the triangles on the inside.

- Stick your thumbs and index fingers under the four flaps.

- Practice flip-flopping your flip-flop so that it opens and closes (Figure 2).

- Now write eight questions or challenges on the eight interior triangles.

- Write the answers beneath each question in the center triangles.

- On the four outside squares name or color four categories (Figure 1).

- Decorate as you like.

To play, ask a friend to choose a color or category on the outside. Spell the category as you flip-flop to each letter (e.g., p-u-r-p-l-e, opening and closing in opposite directions with each letter). Have your friend choose another number or category and repeat the spelling/counting process. Have your friend choose a third number or category, open to the inside, and read the question on that triangle.

Musical Homework

Create a rhythm with your hands and feet to teach to the class. It can be any combination of clapping hands, stamping feet, patting legs, and snapping fingers. You may also include a short phrase, word, or other vocal sound.

When you present your rhythm to the class, you will teach everyone each part, and the class will echo your sounds and movements. For example:

> Clap, clap, clap
> (class echoes)
>
> Pat, pat, pat
> (class echoes)
>
> Clap, clap, pat, pat, snap, snap, snap, "Hey!"
> (class echoes)

Interpersonal Homework

This week your homework is to conduct a survey. You need to interview at least ten people and ask them one of the following questions or one of your own. None of your ten people can be from our class, and at least half of them must be adults. Make some kind of chart or graph to show the results of your survey. Possible questions are listed below:

1. At what age do you think students should decide their own bedtimes? Why did you suggest that age?

2. Do you think there should be year-round schooling with four or five short breaks? Why or why not?

3. What do you think are the most important things a student should learn at school?

130

Part VI: Preparing
Students for Self-
Directed Learning
in a Differentiated
Classroom

4. Do you think all students should learn to speak another language in grade school? Why or why not?

5. At what age do you think students should be allowed to get jobs?

If you don't like any of these questions, create ones of your own; however, get your teacher's approval for your questions before conducting your survey.

After you get your results, make a chart or graph to show your results, and write two conclusions or generalizations from your data.

Intrapersonal Homework

Make a collage of "you." Begin with a picture of yourself in the center and then surround it with things that characterize you. Use pictures cut out from newspapers or magazines, drawings, clip-art, words, poems, or food labels. Include things like your favorite foods, places, sports, animals, activities, or people.

You can find interesting things to cut out in the movie section of the newspaper, the comics, and the headlines. If you do not have any old magazines or newspapers, ask your neighbors if they have any, or peek into a paper recycling bin. Sometimes libraries have magazines they are discarding.

If you use photographs or magazines, obtain permission from the owner before you cut or paste them. If you decide to glue a three-dimensional object onto your collage, make sure the object is not damaged by glue. If you don't want anyone else to see your collage, get a note from a parent stating that you made one. If you don't mind sharing, we will hang the collages in the classroom on Friday and spend some time looking at our collage gallery.

Naturalist Homework

This week, your homework is to make a set of cards with at least five categories. They can be five types of toys, five sports, five kinds of animals or birds or flowers or trees, five buildings, five famous women, five presidents, five classrooms, or any five other similar categories. For each category, you need at least three cards. For example, if you pick five planets, you need at least three information cards for each planet. If you pick five famous African Americans, you need at least three cards about each one.

On Friday, you will have the opportunity to share your cards with your classmates. We will be sorting, categorizing, and making games to play with your cards. You will be adding to your deck of cards over the next few weeks so try to think of an area that will have lots of categories and lots of examples. There are many different birds and flowers and soccer players and countries and famous people and kinds of fruit so those would be good topics. There are not too many kinds of bowling balls or stuffed animals so those might not be very good topics.

If you're not sure which topic to pick, ask your friends or family or me. I would like to approve your topic before you start making your cards just to be sure it will work. Once you have an approved topic, I'll give you fifteen index cards and you can have as many more as you need when you complete those. Have fun!

Differentiating Instruction Using MI Curriculum Units

This section provides teachers with ideas for thematic curriculum units. I do not include complete Multiple Intelligences lessons; instead, I suggest broad topics that may span several weeks or months in study. Each year in my classroom I cover six to eight units. I integrate the discrete disciplines into my units as well as important district and state goals. Although I suggest time frames for covering curriculum units, they are arbitrary and can be adapted to meet the needs of individual classrooms. They create the perfect foundation for differentiating instruction.

How do I choose the themes? Each summer I identify a new theme or two to plan for the coming school year. At the start of the school year I ask my students what they want to study, and together we identify areas that are of interest to them. I also take into account state standards, my district's curriculum, as well as units I have done in the past. From these sources my six to eight yearly units emerge. When time permits I package a thematic topic for easy use at a later time or for sharing with my colleagues. I place my lesson plans and resources in a small box. These thematic "kits" are then easy to store and share.

Part VII Contents

- A List of Thematic Possibilities
- A Curricular Outline, or Mindmap
- Possible MI Lessons for Thematic Unit on Discovery
- Differentiating Instruction with Year-Long Thematic Plans

A List of Thematic Possibilities

Sometimes it is helpful to have a list of possible curricular themes. I like to select a single word and see what complexities and extensions it yields as possible themes. Sometimes I like to take a key word and turn it into a question that guides a curricular unit. For example, the following list includes technological inventions as a possible theme. I might transform these key words into a question, such as "How has technology both helped and hindered humanity?"

Once I've identified a topic, my next step is to outline or mindmap my potential unit, and then to break it down into Multiple Intelligences lesson plans. On the next couple pages I lay the curricular development process for the theme of discovery.

Possible Themes

Discovery

Voyages of discovery

Land journeys of discovery

Flights of discovery

Discovery in space

Microscopic discovery

Subatomic discovery

Futuristic discoveries

Personal discovery

Inventions

Architectural inventions

Mechanical inventions

Electrical inventions

Technological inventions

Industrial inventions

Artistic inventions

Medical inventions

Social inventions

Personal inventions

Challenges

Challenges in science

Challenges in the arts

Challenges in interpersonal relations

Personal challenges

Changes

In the earth

In nature

In the weather

In cultures

In our bodies

In our families

In our friends

Personal changes

Interdependence

In nature

In communities

Among individuals

Between countries

Democracy

In history

In our country

In other countries

In schools

A Curricular Outline, or Mindmap

After I have identified a theme to study, I outline the main subtopics as units of study. I also consider important skills for students to acquire during that unit.

Possible Skills to Teach During the Discovery Unit

Reading, writing, and social-studies skills identified in state standards

Peer feedback

Thinking skills: compare and contrast, analyze, categorize

Historical-research skills

Self-reflection

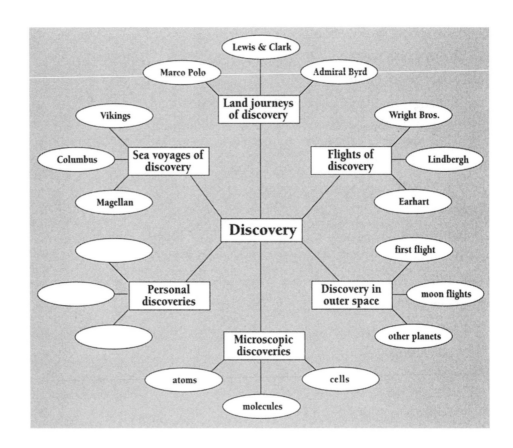

Possible MI Lessons for Thematic Unit on Discovery

Sea Voyages

Activities for Studying the Vikings

Linguistic: identify and read at least three sources of information on Vikings

Logical–mathematical: calculate distances they traveled

Kinesthetic: build model Viking ships

Visual–spatial: illustrate Viking routes on a map

Musical: compose a rhythmic rowing tune

Interpersonal: devise a chain of command on a Viking ship

Intrapersonal: specify the role on a ship one might prefer to assume

Naturalist: design and create a set of explorer trading cards with characteristics of each explorer

Activities for Studying Columbus

Linguistic: read and discuss different perspectives on Columbus

Logical–mathematical: calculate distance problems (rate × time)

Kinesthetic: dramatize his arrival in the Bahamas

Visual–spatial: make a map of Columbus's voyage

Musical: compare fifteenth- and sixteenth-century music

Interpersonal: make plan for peacefully blending cultures

Intrapersonal: specify how to treat Arawaks and why

Naturalist: study types of fish, sea mammals, and sea birds Columbus might have seen

Activities for Studying Magellan

Linguistic: write a speech to a king or queen requesting ships for a long trip

Logical–mathematical: calculate how much food and water needed for a voyage

Kinesthetic activity: climb ropes (to trim sails)

Visual–spatial: draw ships, clothing, or other items from the era

Musical: learn sea chants

Interpersonal: role play the ship's return to Spain

Intrapersonal: maintain a captain's log

Naturalist: compare and contrast features of the Atlantic, the Pacific and the Indian Oceans

Land Journeys

Activities for Studying Marco Polo

Linguistic: read and compare historical accounts of voyages

Logical–mathematical: calculate miles traveled per day, week, month, year during one of Marco Polo's voyages

Kinesthetic: make a board game of his journey

Visual–spatial: draw a scene from one of the countries he visited

Musical: compare Chinese and Italian music of the period

Interpersonal: contrast Chinese and Italian cultures of the period in small groups

Intrapersonal: imitate one of Marco Polo's diary entries

Naturalist: compare and contrast the land voyage and sea voyage from Italy to China

Activities for Studying Lewis and Clark

Linguistic: read script of Lewis and Clark play

Logical–mathematical: divide script; assign roles and tasks

Kinesthetic: construct a set for the play

Visual–spatial: make costumes for the play

Musical: make simple drums to use for musical accompaniment for the play

Interpersonal: reenact the journey to the Pacific

Intrapersonal: reflect on role in the play

Naturalist: catalogue knowledge of plants and animals Lewis and Clark needed to survive

Activities for Studying Admiral Byrd

Linguistic: read selections from books about polar exploration (such as Byrd's *Alone*) and identify the most important things learned from these voyages

Logical–mathematical: describe the scientific studies conducted on his voyages

Kinesthetic: build a contour map of either Pole

Visual–spatial: draw geographic features of either Pole

Musical: create lyrics for a song about a polar journey

Interpersonal: teach one another information learned from Byrd's polar research studies

Intrapersonal: describe how one would respond to living alone in a polar environment

Naturalist: identify the main characteristics of a polar environment, along with its plants and animals

Flights

Activities for Studying the Wright brothers

Linguistic: research lives of the Wright brothers.

Logical–mathematical: calculate scales of their planes; compare them

Kinesthetic: build Popsicle®-stick model planes

Visual–spatial: draw replicas of Wrights' planes

Musical: learn the song "Wild Blue Yonder"

Interpersonal: conduct mock interview with the Wright brothers

Intrapersonal: write about what personal qualities one would need to pioneer such a technological invention

Naturalist: describe how head winds and tail winds affect the takeoff of a plane

Activities for Studying Charles Lindbergh

Linguistic: prepare a brief talk on his historic flight or other aspects of his life

Logical–mathematical: compare the time and distance of his famous journey with those of other explorers

Kinesthetic: Lindbergh was also an inventor; create a mock invention that represents a new technology

Visual–spatial: look at and draw an aerial view of school, community.

Musical: put together a musical collage that represents different events in Lindbergh's life

Interpersonal: discuss different events in his life and their impact on others (e.g., the Lindbergh kidnapping and law, serving as goodwill ambassador, and mapping airline routes with wife Anne Morrow)

Intrapersonal: write about thirty-four hours spent alone

Naturalist: illustrate wave patterns from an aerial perspective

Activities for Studying Amelia Earhart

Linguistic: read Earhart's book and share favorite passages

Logical–mathematical: compare her plans with Magellan's

Kinesthetic: create a series of exercises to do while seated for a long time

Visual–spatial: work with flight-simulation software

Musical: create a song about her feats and disappearance

Interpersonal: identify the qualities that helped her be a pioneer

Intrapersonal: in a mode of choice, reflect on why she is an inspirational figure

Naturalist: investigate the effects clouds can have on passing aircraft

Discoveries in Space

Activities for Studying the First Space Flights

Linguistic: research and teach others about early space flights

Logical–mathematical: compare dimensions of spacecraft with those of planes

Kinesthetic: build clay or plaster replicas of spacecraft

Visual–spatial: make a chart of all manned space flights

Musical: select music for a flight to space

Interpersonal: identify contributions by various countries in early space flights

Intrapersonal: list ten things to take into outer space and explain

Naturalist: investigate changes in air temperature as a rocket is launched from Earth

Activities for Studying the First Lunar Orbits

Linguistic: create a newscast of the first landing on the moon, including Armstrong's speech

Logical–mathematical: calculate speed and distance to reach lunar orbit

Kinesthetic: pantomime moon walking in zero gravity

Visual–spatial: diagram booster, spacecraft, lunar lander

Musical: create background music for news cast of first moon landing

Interpersonal: plan activities for two to three crew members of a small space craft

Intrapersonal: identify personal strengths needed to endure a long space trip

Naturalist: compare and contrast the environments of Earth and the moon

Activities for Studying Discoveries beyond the Solar System

Linguistic: create a list of recent discoveries in outer space

Logical–mathematical: create analogies for large distances

Kinesthetic: dance or role-play shapes of various galaxies

Visual–spatial: make computer graphics of space discoveries

Musical: simulate sounds of outer space (e.g., Big Bang)

Interpersonal: study wormholes and black holes in small groups

Intrapersonal: write feelings about inner and outer space

Naturalist: describe patterns in star clusters and galaxies

Microscopic Discoveries

Activities for Studying Cells

Linguistic: read Madeline L'Engle's *A Wind in the Door* and discuss its scientific accuracy

Logical–mathematical: calculate rates of cells dividing

Kinesthetic: study cells under microscopes

Visual–spatial: watch a videotape or film about microscopic life

Musical: note the sound effects or music used in the video or film to reinforce information

Interpersonal: study different cell discoveries in groups

Intrapersonal: visualize cells dividing in your body

Naturalist: examine and compare different types of cells under

Microscopes, in photos, or on Web sites

Activities for Studying Molecules

Linguistic: read fact sheet on molecular discoveries

Logical–mathematical: extrapolate the numbers of atoms in molecules; e.g., if there are seven atoms in one molecule, how many atoms in five molecules?

Kinesthetic: visit a local science museum that presents information on molecules or molecular discoveries

Visual–spatial: study and draw pictures of a DNA double helix

Musical: improvise music that resembles molecular structures

Interpersonal: compare molecular and human bonding

Intrapersonal: study molecules of different elements

Naturalist: compare and contrast the molecular structures of different compounds

Activities for Studying Atoms

139

Part VII:
Differentiating
Instruction Using MI
Curriculum Units

Linguistic: lecture on atomic discoveries

Logical–mathematical: study the periodic table of the elements

Kinesthetic: build models of atoms with balls, etc.

Visual–spatial: diagram parts of atoms

Musical: compose a song about the parts of an atom

Interpersonal: invite a local scientist to present as a guest speaker

Intrapersonal: choose a favorite element to study and explain how it is
similar to yourself

Naturalist: describe common characteristics of atoms in the rows and
columns of the periodic table of elements

Personal Discoveries

Linguistic: write about a personal discovery

Logical–mathematical: create a timeline of personal discoveries

Kinesthetic: dramatize or dance about a personal discovery

Visual–spatial: make a collage of personal discoveries

Musical: identify and share songs that address personal discoveries

Interpersonal: share personal discoveries in small groups

Intrapersonal: set personal goals for future discoveries

Naturalist: find a new flower, bug, bird, etc.

Differentiating Instruction with Year-Long Thematic Plans

Teachers often ask me which curricular units I enjoy
teaching and which my students enjoy studying. I have
included skeletal outlines of three of my favorite units:
From Quarks to Quasars, Art Around the World, and Our
Only Earth. While the three units are each presented as year-
long, the time frame is in fact flexible. I have taught these
units (in one form or another) in grades one, two, three,
four, five, and six. They could even be adapted for high
school, just as they have been adapted for other grade levels.
These units are built around my state's standards in reading,
writing and the arts, and in math and science/social studies.
You will need to adapt them to your state standards.

Sample Thematic Unit Plan: From Quarks to Quasars

The following curricular unit is divided into three sections: the microcosm, the
human world, and the macrocosm. It integrates common disciplines: language
arts, math, science, social studies, health, art, PE, and music. It is arranged
sequentially but could be taught in reverse order, from macrocosm to microcosm. Showing the short film "Powers of Ten" (available on video or DVD in
most public libraries) is an outstanding way to begin and end the unit.

From Quarks to Quasars

September: The Microcosm

3–4 weeks

Discipline: science
Subatomic particles—quarks, leptons, mesons, etc. [2–3 days]
Atoms—elements, the periodic table [1 week]
Molecules—compounds, molecular bonding [1 week]
Cells—plant and animal cells, cell division [1 week]

October–April: The Human World

5–7 months

Disciplines: health, social studies, language arts
The human body—the brain, the systems [2 weeks]
Human history—prehistory through modern times [2 months]
Human accomplishments—discoveries, inventions, creations
[2 months]
Human cultures—cultures around the world [2 months]
Geography of Earth—continents, mountains, rivers, etc.
[2–3 weeks]

May–June: The Macrocosm

4–6 weeks

Disciplines: science, social studies, language arts
The solar system—planets, asteroids, meteors, etc. [1 week]
The Milky Way Galaxy—stars and constellations [1 week]
The universe—galaxies, black holes, quasars [1 week]
Future advances—cybernetics, technology, what
lies ahead [1 week]

Sample Thematic Unit Plan: Art Around the World

This thematic unit emphasizes social studies and art, but also includes many
language arts, math, science, and music activities. There is no necessary
sequence; two possibilities are a geographical sequence or an historical
sequence. A combination of the two is used below.

Art Around the World

Ancient Art (September)

cave paintings, ancient sculpture
sample activity: making cave-like paintings on brown paper from
grocery bags

Art of Early Civilizations (October)

Sumeria, Egypt, China, India
sample activity: building pyramids or ziggurats

Greek and Roman Art (November)

sculpture, architecture, design
sample activity: doing clay sculpture

African Art (December)

West Africa, South Africa, Central Africa, East Africa
sample activity: making Adinkra quilt (see *Art from Many Hands* in index)

Asian Art (January)

China, Japan, Southeast Asia, India
sample activity: paper making and block printing

European Art (February)

Renaissance, impressionism
sample activity: acrylic painting, watercolor painting

South and Central American Art (March)

Mexico, Guatemala, Peru, Bolivia, Brazil
sample activity: making sand paintings, yarn art

North American Art (April)

Native American art, Colonial arts and crafts, Western art,
sample activity: toy making (e.g., tops)

Modern and Contemporary Art (May)

abstract, expressionism, new kinds of art
sample activity: doing collage, bead work, glass, sculpture

Sample Thematic Unit Plan: Our Only Earth

Our Only Earth is an interdisciplinary unit that addresses local and global challenges. There is no predetermined order to the following units, nor is it necessary to teach every section. Teachers might pick and choose topics that are of the greatest interest to their class. The order suggested below is random; however, in studying these areas most classes find them interdependent and overlapping in many ways.

Our Only Earth

September 15–October 31: **Our Troubled Skies**
air pollution, global warming, the ozone layer

November 1–December 15: **The Ocean Crisis**
water pollution, whaling, land erosion and runoff

January: **Tropical Rain Forests**
deforestation, land degradation, extinction

February: **Endangered Species**
vanishing plants and animals

March: **The Energy Crisis**
problems with production; alternative resources

April: **War: the Global Battlefield**
human conflicts around the world

May: **Our Divided World**
Overpopulation, poverty, and hunger

At the conclusion of each topic, a problem-solving process enables students to suggest and perhaps even implement their solutions. A variety of community-service projects often emerge.

An excellent set of resources for this unit is the *Our Only Earth* series of classroom manuals for global problem solving available through online book venders.

Teachers often want a visual format to guide the development of their curricular plans. Many teachers like to enlarge the following chart to include as much information as possible.

A Thematic Planning Matrix

Theme Focus: _____ Unit: _____

Targeted State Standards: _____

KEY TOPICS OR QUESTIONS	
Desired Outcomes	Interpersonal Activities
Linguistic Activities	Intrapersonal Activities
Logical–Mathematical Activities	Naturalist Activities
Kinesthetic Activities	Assessment Activities
Visual–Spatial Activities	Culminating Activities
Musical Activities	

A Final Word

Throughout this book, I have tried to share some of the ways I use the Theory of Multiple Intelligences to differentiate instruction in my classroom. I think as teachers, however, it is important to develop approaches that work best for you, for your students, and your community.

In looking back over my years of teaching with this model, I want to share a few reflections. I have been willing to do extra planning and create new assessment processes because of the way my students have responded and because of the success I have experienced as a professional. I'd like to explain some of the tangible results I have achieved that motivate me to continue.

What are some of the results of this program?

I have conducted action research projects in my classroom to assess what effects if any this classroom model has on intermediate-aged students. To do the research, I maintained a daily journal with specific entries that recorded the following:

- General daily reflections
- Daily evaluation of how focused or "on-task" students were
- Evaluation of transitions between centers
- Explanation of discipline problems
- Self-assessment—how my teacher-time was used
- Tracking of specific individuals, previously identified as students with serious behavior problems

In addition, I administered a "Classroom Climate Survey" several times during the year, and gathered standardized test data over a period of several years.

The data I gathered revealed the following:

1. Students develop increased responsibility, self-direction, and independence over the course of the year. Although I have not attempted to compare my students with those in other classes, the self-direction and motivation they exhibit has been consistently apparent to literally hundreds of classroom visitors. The students become skilled at developing their own projects, gathering necessary resources and materials, and making well-planned presentations.

2. Discipline problems significantly reduce. Students previously identified as having serious behavior problems show rapid improvement in social skills typically during the first six weeks of school. By mid-year, they are often making important contributions to their groups. And by year's end, they occasionally assume positive leadership roles at the centers.

3. All students develop and apply new skills. In the fall, most students typically describe only one center as their favorite. (Interestingly enough, the distribution among the eight centers is always relatively even.) By mid-year, most identify three to four favorite centers. By year's end, nearly every student identifies at least three centers as favorites. Moreover, they all make multimodal presentations of their independent projects which include songs, skits, visuals, poems, games, surveys, puzzles, and group participation activities—the skills they are developing at the eight centers.

4. Cooperative learning skills improve in all students. Since so much of the center work is collaborative, students become highly skilled at listening, helping each other, sharing leadership in different activities, accommodating group changes, and introducing new classmates to the program. They learn not only to respect each other, but also to appreciate and call upon the unique gifts and abilities of their classmates.

5. Academic achievement has improved as measured by both classroom and standardized tests. State scores are at or above local, state and national averages in all areas. Retention is high on classroom year-end tests. Methods for recalling information are predominately musical, visual, and kinesthetic, indicating the power of Differentiated Instruction and influence of working through the different intelligences. I have observed students who were previously unsuccessful in school become high-achievers in new areas.

In summary, it is clear that students' learning improves. Many students say they enjoy school for the first time. As the school year progresses, new skills emerge. Some students discover musical abilities, artistic, literary, mathematical, and other capacities. Some become skilled leaders. In addition, self-confidence and motivation increase significantly. Finally, students develop responsibility, self-reliance and independence as they take an active role in shaping their own learning experiences.

What is the teacher's role in a Differentiated MI program?

One interesting consequence of a student-centered classroom such as this is the role of the teacher. While the majority of students are at work in the centers and on projects, my time is spent with individuals or small groups. I help students learn new skills, tutor those with reading or math difficulties, assist gifted students with challenging activities, and work with small groups to design structures, create dances, and plan projects. Additionally, I often confer with individual students, evaluating their work, suggesting opportunities for improvement, and giving positive feedback. So, my role has become that of facilitator, guide, and resource provider. My relationships with students are more personal and I am gratified by their individual accomplishments.

Not only has my role changed, but I have also developed new competencies as a result of teaching in a such an environment. I have learned to observe my students from multiple perspectives. I have become more accomplished at preparing for diverse methods of learning and gathering resources to facilitate learning that is center- and project-based. I also find that I am working *with* my students, rather than *for* them, exploring what they explore, discovering what they discover, and often learning what they learn. My satisfaction is gleaned from my students' enthusiasm for learning and their independence, rather than from their test scores and ability to sit quietly. Perhaps most importantly, because of planning for such diverse modes of learning, I have become more creative and multimodal in my own thinking and learning. I sometimes wonder who is changing the most, the students or myself?

Why is a Multiple Intelligences model of Differentiated Instruction successful?

The program has been successful not only in my classroom but in hundreds more around the country. There seem to be two reasons for the success. First, every student has an opportunity to specialize and excel in at least one area of human intelligence. Usually, however, it is three or four. Since I began this program, there has not been a single student unable to find an area of specialty and success. Second, each student is learning subject matter in multiple ways and has a variety of opportunities to understand and retain academic information. Moreover, because of the input students have into the program, their learning experiences are personally meaningful.

Many student needs are met through differentiated instruction. Their intellectual needs are met through the constant challenges in their daily activities. Emotional needs are met at times by working closely with others and at other times by working independently. Ultimately, I believe that students working in an MI environment develop new strengths and come to better understand and appreciate themselves as individuals. Because of the skills the students develop, they have multiple abilities to pursue their interests long after they leave the classroom. And that has always been my goal as an educator: to inspire a love of learning in each child I teach.

References

Armstrong, Thomas. *In Their Own Way.* Los Angeles: Tarcher, 1987.

Benzie, Teresa. *A Moving Experience: Dance for Lovers of Children and the Child Within.* Tucson: Zephyr, 1987.

Blood-Patterson, Peter. *Rise Up Singing.* Bethlehem, PA: Sing Out Corp., 1988.

Brookes, Mona. *Drawing with Children.* Los Angeles: Tarcher, 1986.

Burns, Marilyn. *A Collection of Math Lessons, Books 1–3.* White Plains, NY: Math Solutions Publications, Cuisenaire Co. of America, 1987.

Campbell, Linda. *Mindful Learning: 101 Proven Strategies for Student and Teacher Success.* Thousand Oaks, CA: Corwin, 2003.

Campbell, Linda, and Bruce Campbell. *Multiple Intelligences and Student Achievement: Success Stories from Six Schools.* Alexandria, VA: ASCD, 1999.

Campbell, Linda et al. *Our Only Earth: A Global Problem-Solving Series.* Tucson: Zephyr, 1990.

Campbell, Linda et al. *Teaching & Learning through Multiple Intelligences.* Needham Heights, MA: Allyn & Bacon, 1994.

Csikszentmihalyi, Mihaly. *Flow: The Psychology of Optimal Experience.* New York: Cambridge University Press, 1990.

Dunn, Rita and Kenneth. *Teaching Students through Their Individual Learning Styles: A Practical Approach.* Reston, VA: Prentice Hall, 1978.

Educational Testing Service and Harvard Project Zero. *Arts PROPEL: An Introductory Handbook.* Harvard Graduate School of Education: Cambridge, 1991.

Gardner, Howard. *Frames of Mind: The Theory of Multiple Intelligences.* New York: Basic Books, 1983.

Gardner, Howard. *Multiple Intelligences: The Theory in Practice.* New York: Basic Books, 1993.

Gardner, Howard. *Multiple Intelligences: New Horizons.* New York: Perseus, 2006.

Gilbert, Anne. *Teaching the Three R's through Movement.* New York: MacMillan, 1989.

Gilbert, Anne. *Creative Dance for All Ages.* Reston, VA: American Alliance for Health, Physical Education, Recreation and Dance, 1992.

Gregory, Gayle. *Differentiated Instructional Strategies in Practice.* Thousand Oaks, CA: Corwin, 2003.

Koch, Kenneth and Kate Farrel. *Talking to the Sun.* New York: Henry Holt, 1985.

Koch, Kenneth. *Wishes, Lies, and Dreams: Teaching Poetry to Children.* New York: Henry Holt, 1979.

Lewis, Barbara. *The Kids Guide to Social Action.* Minneapolis: Free Spirit Publishing, 1998.

Liem, Tik. *Invitations to Science Inquiry.* Chino Hills, CA: Science Inquiry Enterprises, 1990.

Marzano, Robert J. *What Works in Schools.* Alexandria, VA: ASCD, 2003.

Marzano, Robert J. *Classroom Instruction That Works: Research-Based Strategies for Increasing Student Achievement.* Alexandria, VA: ASCD, 2004.

Merriam-Webster's Visual Dictionary. New York: Merriam-Webster, 2006.

Ruef, Kerry. *The Private Eye: (5X) Looking/Thinking by Analogy.* Seattle, WA: The Private Eye Project, 1992.

Schuman, Jo. *Art from Many Hands: Multicultural Art Projects.* Worcester, MA: Davis Publications, 2005.

Tomlinson, Carol Ann. *The Differentiated Classroom.* Alexandria, VA: ASCD, 1995.

Tomlinson, Carol Ann. *How to Differentiate Instruction in Mixed-Ability Classrooms.* Alexandria, VA: ASCD, 1999.

Tomlinson, Carol Ann et al. "Differentiating instruction in response to student readiness, interest, and learning profile in academically diverse classrooms: A review of literature." *Journal for the Education of the Gifted,* 27(2/3), 199–145: 2003.

Wiseman, Ann. *Making Things, Books 1 & 2.* Boston: Little, Brown & Co., 1997.

Wolfe, Patricia. *Brain Matters.* Alexandria, VA: ASCD, 2001.

Wormelli, R. *Fair Isn't Always Equal.* Westerville, OH: Stenhouse, 2006.

Index